The Charlie Brown Dictionary

The Charlie Brown Dictionary

by Charles M. Schulz

Based on THE RAINBOW DICTIONARY
by Wendell W. Wright, Ph.D.,
assisted by Helene Laird.

WORLD PUBLISHING
TIMES MIRROR
NEW YORK

PRENTICE-HALL, INC., Englewood Cliffs, N.J.

Acknowledgment is made to Lee Mendelson—
Bill Melendez TV Productions,
for illustrations from the television productions,
It's The Great Pumpkin, Charlie Brown;
"He's Your Dog, Charlie Brown!";
"You're In Love, Charlie Brown";
It Was A Short Summer, Charlie Brown;
Play It Again, Charlie Brown; and Charlie Brown's All-Stars,
all by Charles M. Schulz and
published by The World Publishing Company.
Acknowledgement is also made to George O'Hara,
acquiring editor, for enthusiastic support in this project.

Library of Congress Catalog Card Number: 72-12135
ISBN 0-13-084269-9

Printed in The United States of America.

2 3 4 5 6 7 8 9 10

An Explanation

THE CHARLIE BROWN DICTIONARY is a new dictionary based on a classic model —*The Rainbow Dictionary,* published originally in 1947 and in a new copyright edition in 1959, and a bestseller in its field since publication.

The present dictionary is new in both its illustrations and its definitions, but the vocabulary is largely that of *The Rainbow Dictionary,* with additions and deletions reflecting changes in the language that children hear, speak and read. The concept of the dictionary also remains unchanged: youngsters should *enjoy* the use of a dictionary. They should find it a source of pleasure so that, as they grow, they will easily turn to more advanced dictionaries as a source of knowledge.

As we stated in the introduction to the original edition, children grow up in a world of bewildering words. From the time they speak their first simple syllables to adulthood, when their vocabulary has increased to thousands of words, their successful adjustment in life is largely dependent, so educators have found, on their knowledge of words. Intellectual growth, broad cultural development, the capacity for expression, and further learning by reading all come through the assimilation of the meaning of words. A dictionary for children, therefore, is as important a reference book as a dictionary for adults—perhaps even more important. Its scope must naturally be small to keep it within the child's power to absorb and his range of interest, but its construction must be as painstaking and far more imaginative than the construction of the ponderous volumes used by grown-ups.

THE CHARLIE BROWN DICTIONARY contains 2,400 entries, consisting of both main entries and related forms, which children use in speaking, hear on television and recognize when reading. The words chosen are those that occurred most frequently in a consolidation of eight word lists for children from five to eight years old. Five of these word lists are standard published lists; one is from the unpublished research of the author of *The Rainbow Dictionary,* Wendell W. Wright; and two were made expressly for that publication under Dr. Wright's direction. Of the last two, one was based on the most commonly read children's books, the other on an analysis of the comic pages of standard Sunday newspapers sampled over a period of one year.

The vocabulary which finally evolved from this extensive research is thus based almost entirely on frequency. This strict adherence to frequency in determining the choice of words was felt to be by far the best and most practical system for a children's dictionary. Consistency of style, in fact, has been disregarded wherever it seemed that to do so would be helpful to the young reader. The parts of verbs given, for instance, are those most frequently used, rather than any regular number of parts chosen merely for the fact that they are, say, the present, past and future tenses. In some instances four or five parts of a verb will be listed, in others only one or two. The same rule governed the inclusion of plural forms of nouns, and of comparative and superlative forms of adjectives. If children use them frequently, they are entered in the vocabulary; if not, they are omitted. This principle creates a few instances in which the noun appears only in its plural form.

No word has been included which has not been defined in some way, either within the definition, in the illustration, or in another entry. In brief, the object has been to put every word where the child will naturally look for it, to include every word which he will be likely to look for, and to define every word included. It has been assumed that in some instances the youngster will be read to; that pre-readers will be given this book, and will want to hear the words that "go with" a particular picture of Snoopy or Charlie Brown or Lucy. Therefore the definitions are written so that they can be comfortably read or read aloud.

Many methods have been used to help children to learn the meanings of words. The principal methods are:

1. The picture with its caption—delineating an object, illustrating an action, or illuminating an idea:

   full—Lucy's basket is **full**. There is no room in it for anything more. It cannot hold any more.

2. The simple explanation of the meaning of the word:

   finish—We will **finish** our work very soon. We will **come to the end** of our work very soon.

3. The use of the word in a sentence with additional facts to help clarify its meaning:

   face—The front part of your head is your **face.** Your eyes, your nose, your cheeks and your mouth are parts of your face.

4. The use of the word and a synonymous word or phrase in two otherwise identical sentences. (Synonyms were not used unless they were simpler and more readily understandable to the child

than the word being defined, and unless they too were defined in their proper place in the alphabet.)

leave—Sally watches Charlie Brown **leave** the house. Sally watches Charlie Brown **go away** from the house.

5. The use of the word with its antonym:

dirty—Pig-Pen's hands and face and clothes are **dirty.** Pig-Pen is **not clean.**

Very frequently two or three of these ways have been used in defining one word.

The style of language throughout the book is simple. The expressions are those of children, and the ideas and situations are within the range of the common experience of children.

The pictures by Charles M. Schulz are not only enticing, but are also sparkling in their clarity. No one can communicate the desire for food quite as eloquently as Snoopy; Lucy's expressive face often "writes" the definition for the younger reader. One can be sure that even toddlers will expectantly, happily turn the pages to see the Peanuts gang.

THE CHARLIE BROWN DICTIONARY, then, is a picture book and a book of knowledge, but above all a book of words and their meanings.

THE PUBLISHERS

The Charlie Brown Dictionary

A a

a Linus has **a** ball. Linus has **one** ball.

able Lucy is **able** to read.
Lucy **can** read. Lucy **knows how** to read.

aboard The kids are lined up to climb **aboard** the bus.
The kids are lined up to get **on** the bus.

When we go on or into a train, plane, ship or bus that will take us somewhere, we call it going aboard.

about Frieda has **about** as many friends as Peppermint Patty.
Frieda has **nearly the same number** of friends as Peppermint Patty.

Schroeder is **about** as tall as Charlie Brown.
Schroeder is **almost** as tall as Charlie Brown.

This book tells **about** words we use.
What we read in this book **has to do with** words.

I am **about** to go to bed.
I am going to bed **in a minute or two.**

---

above Linus is standing **above** Lucy.
Linus is standing **over** Lucy.

He is **higher** than she is.

---

absent Why was Franklin **absent** from school today?
Why was Franklin **not at** school today? Perhaps he was not there because he had a cold.

---

accident

Bonk! The baseball hit Lucy on the top of her head.
It was an **accident.**
It **did not happen on purpose. No one expected** the ball to hit her.

When something unpleasant happens by mistake or by chance —when we break a dish, or when one car hits another—we often call it an accident.

ache

Charlie Brown has a stomach **ache.**
Charlie Brown's stomach **hurts.**
He feels **pain** in his stomach.

When you have a toothache, it means that you have a pain in your tooth. It might not go away until the dentist makes you feel better.

---

across Snoopy is running **across** the street.
Snoopy is running **from one side** of the street **to the other.**

---

act Sometimes Lucy does not **act** pleasantly with her friends.
Sometimes Lucy does not **behave** or **do things** nicely.

In the play at school, you are supposed to **act** like a dog.
You must **make believe** you are a dog, and do some of the things a dog does. You will bark and run around on your hands and feet.

---

add If you **add** one and one, you have two. To **add** is to **put together.**
If you **put together** one block with another block, you have two blocks.

Some people **add** sugar to their cereal to make it sweet.
Some people **put on** sugar to make their cereal sweet.

address Your **address** tells us **where you live**—the number of your house or building, the name of the street, the name of the city and the name of the state. If your friends know your address, they will know just where to visit you or write to you.

---

afraid

Snoopy is **afraid** that the boy will take his dinner away.
Snoopy is **worried** that his dish will be taken away.

He barks at the boy, and for a moment the boy is **afraid.**
He is **scared** that Snoopy will bite him. But Snoopy doesn't bite.

---

after Violet is running **after** Charlie Brown.
Violet is running **behind** Charlie Brown and **trying to catch** him.

Charlie Brown and Violet are racing to see who can get to a certain place first. It looks as if Charlie Brown will get there first.
Violet will get there **after** him.
Violet will get there **later** than Charlie Brown.

---

afternoon **The time between twelve o'clock noon and evening** is called the **afternoon.**

---

afterward Franklin is going to school now, and **afterward** he is going to play baseball.
Later, after school is over for the day, Franklin will play ball.

again Please read this **again.**
Please read this **one more time.**

---

against

Lucy is leaning **against** Schroeder's piano.
Lucy is stretched out beside the piano, and her arms and shoulders are **touching** it.

We played **against** each other in the baseball game.
We played **on different sides** in the baseball game.

---

age Two of the three kids are the same **age,** but the third is younger.
Charlie Brown's little sister Sally is not as old as Charlie Brown or Linus. Sally hasn't had as many birthdays as Charlie Brown or Linus have had.

What is your **age?**
How old are you?

---

ago The Bible was written long **ago.**
The Bible was written long **before now.**

---

agree Lucy and Charlie Brown rarely **agree.**
Lucy and Charlie Brown do not often **think alike.**

Will Lucy **agree** to do it?
Will Lucy **be willing** to do it?

Too much candy will not **agree** with me.
Too much candy will not **be good** for me.

ahead Charlie Brown, Lucy and Violet are standing in line to buy tickets to a movie.

Violet is **ahead** of Lucy.
Violet is **in front of** Lucy and will buy her ticket before Lucy does.
Lucy is **ahead** of Charlie Brown.
Lucy is **in front of** Charlie Brown.

---

air Fish live in the water, but we live in the **air.** **Air** is **what we breathe.** The airplane flies through the air. We blow air into balloons. We do not see air, but if we wave our hands near our face, we can feel the air moving against our face.

---

airplane An **airplane** is a **machine that flies.** There are many different kinds of airplanes.

---

airport The **airport** is a special place **where airplanes land and take off.** People get on and off the planes at an airport. Planes are cleaned and made ready for their flights at an airport.

alarm When the **alarm** goes off at the fire station, the **loud noise** warns the firemen that there is a fire somewhere.

The **alarm** clock has a bell that suddenly rings to **signal** that it's time to get up.

We say that a sudden noise **alarms** us. It makes us think that something may be wrong. It makes us look for danger.

---

alike

Woodstock and the bird that follows him look very much **alike.**
Woodstock and the bird look very much **the same.**

---

alive This plant is **alive.**

This plant is dead.

all

Charlie Brown is **all** wet.
Charlie Brown was drinking from the water fountain, and the water splashed over **every part** of his body.
When we say that we want to eat **all** of a cookie, we want to eat **the whole thing.**

---

allow Will Charlie Brown **allow** Lucy to use his bat?
Will Charlie Brown **let** Lucy use his bat?

---

almost Linus is **almost** as tall as Lucy.
Linus is **nearly** as tall as Lucy.

---

alone Snoopy is all **alone.**
Snoopy is **not with anyone.**

Can the baby dress herself **alone?**
Can the baby dress herself **without anyone** to help?

---

aloud When we **talk,** we speak **aloud.** When we whisper, we do not speak aloud.

---

alphabet A word is made of letters, and **all the letters together** are called the **alphabet.** The first three letters of the alphabet are A, B and C.

---

already Snoopy has learned to skate **already.**
Snoopy has learned to skate **before this time.**

also

Lucy is wearing roller skates. Snoopy is wearing them **also.**
Snoopy is wearing them **too.**

---

although They played baseball **although** it was raining.
They played baseball **even though** it was raining.

---

always Snoopy is **always** hungry.
Snoopy is hungry **all the time.**

American

Charlie Brown is looking at the **American** flag at the top of the pole. Charlie Brown is an **American.** People who live in the United States of America are called Americans. The fifty stars in the flag are a way of showing us that there are fifty states in America. The colors of the American flag are red, white and blue.

among

Charlie Brown is **among** the kids who are ready to play baseball.
Charlie Brown is **in the middle of** the group of kids who are ready to play baseball.

Among the special things the kids are wearing to play baseball are a catcher's mask and baseball hats.
Mixed in with the things the kids are wearing to play baseball are a mask and hats.

---

an Sally put **an** egg and **an** onion on the table.
Sally put **one** egg and **one** onion on the table.

---

and Violet will eat dinner **and** then go to bed.
Violet will eat dinner. **Also,** Violet will then go to bed.

---

angry Lucy is **angry.** Lucy **feels mean.**
Lucy has the **feeling that she would like to fight with someone** or **make someone unhappy.**

Sometimes when we're angry, we say we are "mad."

---

animal

A **living creature** that is not some sort of plant is an **animal.**

When we talk about animals, we usually think of four-legged creatures, like lions or elephants or dogs. Snoopy is an animal who thinks he's a person.

ankle

Snoopy and Woodstock are playing hockey.

Oops! Snoopy hurt his **ankle.** Your ankle is the **part of your body between your foot and your lower leg.**

---

annoy Lucy will **annoy** Schroeder if she talks while he is playing the piano. Lucy will **make** Schroeder **a little angry.**

---

another Linus built a snowman. Then Linus built **another** one. Linus built **one more.**

I want **another** kind of candy. I want **a different** kind of candy.

---

answer

When the telephone rings, Charlie Brown will **answer** it. When the phone rings, Charlie Brown will **pick it up, speak into it, and listen.**

When your mother calls, you **answer.** You let her know you heard her. You **reply,** "What is it, Mom?"

If the question is, "How much is two and two?", the **answer** is, "Four."

ant An **ant** is one kind of **bug.**

any You may have **any** flower from the garden.
You may have **one** flower that you choose from the garden.

Do you have **any** toys to give to the hospital?
Do you have **some** toys to give to the hospital?

anybody Did **anybody** see my dog?
Did **any person** see my dog?

anyone May **anyone** play here?
May **any person** play here? May **anybody** play here?

anything You may have **anything** on the table.
You may have **any one** of the things that are on the table.

Lucy's new dress isn't **anything** like Sally's.
Lucy's new dress isn't **at all** like Sally's.

anywhere Snoopy will go **anywhere** that Charlie Brown goes.
Snoopy will go **any place** that Charlie Brown goes.

apartment We live in an **apartment.** Our home is in one part of an apartment building. There are many apartments in our building. A different family lives in each apartment.

appear In the spring the leaves **appear** on the trees.
In the spring the leaves **come out** on the trees.

I will turn on the television set, and in a moment the picture will **appear.**
In a moment the picture will **come into sight.**

---

apple

An **apple** is one kind of **fruit.** It is round and usually red or green. Apples grow on trees. Charlie Brown seems surprised to have caught an apple in his glove.

April **April** is the fourth month of the year. It comes in the spring. It has thirty days. The first day of April is April Fool's Day, when kids play tricks on one another.

---

apron Snoopy wears an **apron** while he cleans the house. An apron is a **little skirt** or **piece of cloth worn in front** of us **to keep our clothes clean** while we're working.

aquarium Charlie Brown and Sally are watching the fish in an **aquarium.**

An aquarium is a **water-filled bowl or tank** in which fish are kept.

---

arm Lucy hurt her **arm.** Her arm includes her hand, her wrist, her elbow, and the part between her elbow and her shoulder.

---

army An **army** is made up of **men who are called soldiers.** They must fight if their country is at war.

---

around Snoopy wears a collar **around** his neck. Snoopy wears a collar that **circles** his neck.

arrive Peppermint Patty will **arrive** tomorrow.
Peppermint Patty will **come here** tomorrow.

---

arrow An **arrow** is a pointed stick. Indians hunted with a bow and arrows.

---

ask **When you want something from someone,** you **ask** for it. You say, "May I have it, please?"

When I **ask** someone the time, I **question** him about the time.

---

asleep Linus is **asleep** in his bed.

Linus is **not awake.** His eyes are closed and he is dreaming.

---

atom **Atoms** are the **tiny bits that all things are made of.** An atom is so small we cannot see it.

---

attention Frieda is proud of the way she can jump rope. But Charlie Brown and Linus are not paying **attention.** They are not **watching carefully** while Frieda jumps.

August **August** is the **eighth month** of the year. It comes in the summer. It has thirty-one days.

---

aunt **My father's sister** is my **aunt.** **My mother's sister** is my aunt. **My uncle's wife** is my aunt too.

---

automobile An **automobile** is a **machine on wheels.** We sit in it and ride in it from one place to another. The person who makes the auto move is the driver.

---

autumn **Autumn** is one of the four seasons of the year. Between summer and winter we have autumn. Autumn is also called the fall. In the autumn the leaves fall from some trees.

awake Charlie Brown went to bed, but he is **awake.**
Charlie Brown went to bed, but he is **not asleep.**
He can't sleep because he is thinking about the little red-haired girl.

B b

baby

A **baby** is a **very young child.** Charlie Brown's **baby** sister doesn't seem very happy. Can you guess why?

back Someone has thrown a snowball at Lucy and—wop!—it hits her on the **back** of her head. The **back** of something is the **part behind.**

Now Lucy may throw the snowball **back.** When something **returns to the place** from which **it started,** it goes back. If you go back to your room, you are returning to the room from which you came.

backward

Poor Linus has fallen **backward** over a big pumpkin. He has fallen **on his back.** Maybe Linus fell because he stepped backward instead of forward.

---

bad Something **bad** is **not good.** A bad dream is a dream that isn't good. It is a bad dream, or a dream that makes you afraid.

bag

It's Halloween, and the kids are all dressed up in costumes. Each one carries a **bag** for treats.

A **bag** is usually made of paper or cloth and **is used for carrying things.** A bigger and heavier bag that is used for carrying clothes on a trip is called a suitcase.

---

baggage

Snoopy has packed his suitcases and put them with his golf bag, his sleeping bag, his tennis racket and all the other **things** he needs **for a** summer vacation **trip.**

All of this together is called his **baggage.** You usually take baggage with you when you travel somewhere.

---

bake Mother can **bake** a cake.
Mother can **cook** a cake in the oven.

bakery A person whose job it is to bake cakes, bread and pies is called a baker. He works in a **bakery.**

---

ball

Snoopy and Lucy are playing with a **ball.** This ball is round and made of rubber, and so it bounces and rolls.

---

balloon Sally Brown has a **balloon.** It is made of rubber, and when the little rubber bag is filled with air, it grows larger and larger.

Sometimes a balloon is filled with too much air, and can't stretch any more. Then it breaks.

---

banana A **banana** is one kind of **fruit.** It has a yellow skin and a soft, white inside that's good to eat.

band The kids have a musical **band.** The kids play music together for their own fun and for other people. The big stringed instrument Snoopy plays is called a bass fiddle.

Charlie Brown plays the guitar. Pig-Pen plays the drums.

A **rubber band** is a small circle of rubber that stretches. I held five envelopes together by putting a rubber band around them.

---

bank A **bank** is a **place in which to keep money.** There are little toy banks and there are banks so big that they fill entire buildings.
A **bank** is the land that is on the sides of a river or stream.

---

bar A **bar** is a **long piece of wood or metal.** The bars of a cage are close together so that the animal that is inside cannot get out.

---

bare

Lucy and a friend are running in the grass with **bare** feet.
When your feet are bare, they have **no coverings on** them—no socks and no shoes.

---

bark The noise made by a dog is his **bark.** Snoopy's bark sounds like this, **"Arf! Arf! Arf!"**

The **bark** of a tree is its outside skin. The bark is like a coat for the tree.

baseball **Baseball** is a game with nine players on each of two teams. The teams play against each other. One important part of baseball is to hit a ball with a bat. Poor Snoopy. He's just missed three balls, and so he's out.

---

basement The lowest part of a building is sometimes called the **basement.** The basement is usually partly below the ground. Not every house has a basement. Sometimes the basement is called the **cellar.**

---

basket

Snoopy hops along like a rabbit, carrying a **basket.** Baskets are used to carry small things, and are often made of wood or straw.

basketball **Basketball** is a game played by two teams of five players each. They try to throw a large ball through two rings called the baskets.

bat

Beside Charlie Brown is his **bat.** A baseball bat is used to hit the ball in a baseball game. Why do you think Charlie Brown looks sad? Maybe he couldn't hit the ball with his bat.

A certain little **animal** that looks like a mouse with wings is called a **bat.** Bats fly about at night.

bath Charlie Brown got so tied up with his kite string that he had to take the kite with him when he got into his **bath.** When we take a bath, we bathe—we wash our whole bodies.

bathroom The **bathroom** is the room in which we bathe. I brush my teeth in the bathroom. Daddy shaves in the bathroom.

---

bathtub I take my bath in a **bathtub.**
I fill a big tub with water, sit in it and wash all over.

---

beach A **beach** is the **sandy land** at the edge of the water.

Charlie Brown and Linus are running on the beach. Later they'll swim in the ocean.

---

beans **Beans** are a **vegetable** grown in gardens. Some beans that are good to eat are lima beans and string beans.

---

bear A **bear** is a large, heavy animal with brown, black or white fur.

---

beard A **beard** is **the hair growing on the lower part of the face.**
Santa Claus has a long white beard.

---

beast A **beast** is an animal.

---

beat To play a drum, you **beat** it with a drumstick.
To play a drum, you **hit** it with a drumstick.

Pig-Pen **beats** the drum.
He **strikes** it, and we hear low, loud sounds.

Can you **beat** him in the race?
Can you **win** the race against him?

beautiful Charlie Brown thinks the little red-haired girl is **beautiful.**

Charlie Brown thinks the little red-haired girl is **very nice to look at.**

Beautiful music is very nice to hear.

---

became The seed **became** a plant. The seed **grew** into a plant.

---

because Linus is crying **because** Snoopy cut up his blanket and made it into a little coat.

Linus is crying **for the reason that** Snoopy cut up his blanket and made it into a little coat.

---

bed Linus sits on his **bed,** already almost fast asleep. Lucy has to help him take his shoes and socks off.

A bed is a piece of furniture on which we can stretch out comfortably and sleep.

bedroom The **bedroom** is a room for sleeping. Linus's bed is in his bedroom.

---

bedtime Linus's **bedtime** is eight o'clock.
Linus's **time to go to bed** is eight o'clock.

---

bee A **bee** is a black and yellow **bug** with wings. The bee buzzes. Bees make honey.

---

beet A **beet** is a **vegetable** that grows in the garden. We eat the dark red root of the beet after it is cooked.

---

before Snoopy walks along **before** Linus.
Snoopy walks along **in front of** Linus.

The children play games **before** school starts.
The children play games **earlier** than school starts.

beg

"I **beg** you to tell me where you hid my blanket," Linus says to Lucy. To beg is to do more than just ask, because the answer is very important.

---

begin Now let's **begin** to draw a picture.
Now let's **start** to draw a picture.

began Yesterday the baby **began** to walk.
Yesterday the baby **started** to walk.

---

behave The teacher told Pig-Pen to **behave** nicely.
The teacher told Pig-Pen to **act** nicely.

---

behind Lucy stands **behind** Linus to watch television.
Lucy stands **in back of** Linus to watch television.
He is in front of her.

believe I **believe** that story.
I think that story is true.

belong Who does this book **belong** to?
Who **owns** this book? Franklin does. It **belongs** to him.

below When something is **below** you, it is **not as high up** as you. The baseball field is below Charlie Brown. It is not above him or even with him. He looks down at it.

belt A **belt** is worn around the waist. Father wears a leather belt to hold up his trousers. Mother has a gold belt to wear with dresses and skirts.

bench Charlie Brown sits and waits on a **bench.** A **bench** is usually made of wood and is long enough to be used as a seat by several people at the same time.

A work bench is a high wooden table you can stand at while hammering, sawing and doing other jobs.

bend Why does Woodstock's flower **bend?**
Why doesn't Woodstock's flower stand straight?
It leans over. It is **bent.**
Can you **bend** down and touch the floor?
Can you **lean over** and touch the floor?

---

beneath

Violet is **beneath** the umbrella.
Violet is **under** the umbrella.
Snoopy is **beneath** the umbrella too.

---

berry A **berry** is a small juicy **fruit.** There are many kinds of **berries.** Some that are good to eat are strawberries, blackberries and raspberries.

---

beside Linus is standing **beside** Lucy beneath the umbrella.
Linus is standing **next to** Lucy beneath the umbrella.

besides What books to you have **besides** this one?
What books do you have **other than** this one?

---

best I like fruit, ice cream and cookies, but I like fruit **best.**
I like fruit, ice cream and cookies, but I like fruit **most.**

Schroeder's writing is the best in the class.
No one else in the class writes as well as Schroeder.

---

better Schroeder's writing is **better** than Linus's.
Linus's writing is not as good as Schroeder's.

Charlie Brown had a stomach ache yesterday, but today he feels **better.**
Charlie Brown had a stomach ache yesterday, but today he feels **not so sick.**

---

between Lucy stands **between** her friends.
Lucy stands **in the middle,** with a friend on each side.

beyond **Beyond** the canoes and the water are trees and tents.
Farther away than the canoes and the water are trees and tents.

Bible The **Bible** is a book that tells about God.

---

bicycle I like to ride from one place to another on my **bicycle.** My bicycle moves on two wheels, and I make the wheels turn.

A tricycle has three wheels.

big Compared to his baby sister, Charlie Brown is quite **big.** Something big is **large.**

bigger Charlie Brown is **bigger** than his sister.
Charlie Brown is **larger** than his sister.

biggest Who is the **biggest** person you know?
Who is the **largest** person you know?

---

bill A **bird's mouth** is called his **bill.** Woodstock's mouth is his bill.

My mother bought a new dress. She did not pay for it when she bought it. Later the store sent her a **bill** for it. The bill is a **piece of paper that tells** her **how much money she must pay.**

A dollar **bill** is money.

---

bird

Woodstock is a little **bird.**

Birds have two wings, feathers and a bill. Most birds can fly. Birds are born from eggs. Two big birds are eagles and hawks. Two little birds are sparrows and swallows.

---

birthday Today is my friend's seventh **birthday.**
My friend is seven years old today. She was born on this day of the month seven years ago.

bit Frieda used a **bit** of cloth to make a doll dress.
Frieda used a **small piece** of cloth to make a doll dress.

---

bite Snoopy grabbed Linus by the leg, but Snoopy was careful not to **bite** him.
Snoopy grabbed Linus by the leg, but Snoopy was careful not to **cut** Linus **with his teeth.**

bit I **bit** the cookie. I **took a bite** of the cookie with my teeth.

---

bitter Some things taste **bitter.** They have a sour taste. They do **not** taste **sweet.** The outside part of an orange tastes bitter.

---

black Franklin is Charlie Brown's little **black** friend. He is talking to Charlie Brown on the telephone. Black is a **color.** Black is also another word for **Negro,** a person with dark skin. The words in this book are black.

---

blackboard
Charlie Brown is writing on the **blackboard.** The special thing about a blackboard is that you can write on it with chalk and then clean it off. Most blackboards are black, but some are green. Yet people still call them blackboards.

blame Do you **blame** me because the bicycle is broken?
Do you **think it was my fault** that the bicycle is broken?

I was not to blame.
It was not my fault.

---

blanket Snoopy and Charlie Brown are warm and comfortable under the **blanket.** A blanket is a **cover** you use when you are in bed. It keeps out the cold and keeps you warm. Most blankets are made of wool or cotton.

---

blaze When wood burns, it makes a **blaze.**
When wood burns, it makes a **flame.**

blind The girl is **blind.**
The girl **cannot see.**

---

block My friend and I live on the same **block.**
My friend and I live on the same **street.**

We play with blocks. They are made of wood, and on each of their six sides there is a letter or a picture.

---

bloom Snoopy is rushing past a plant in **bloom.** When a plant **has flowers,** we say it is in bloom.

Many plants bloom in the spring.
Many plants have flowers in the spring.

blooming Some of the plants are **blooming** now.
Some of the plants are **growing new flowers** now.

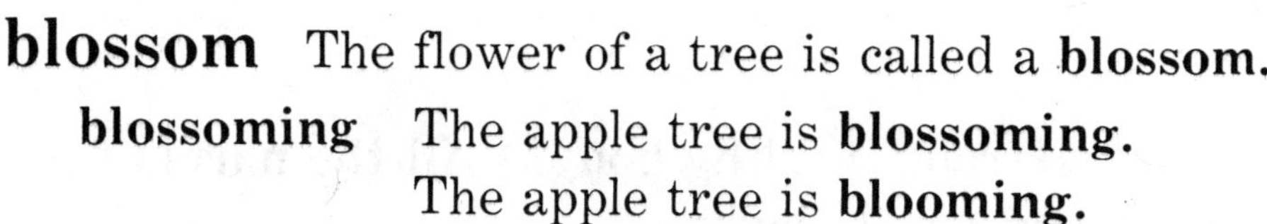

blossom The flower of a tree is called a **blossom.**

blossoming The apple tree is **blossoming.**
The apple tree is **blooming.**

---

blow

Snoopy can **blow** the book right out of Linus's hands.
Snoopy can **make air go out of his mouth** so fast that the air pushes the book right out of Linus's hands.
When you blow up a balloon, you put air into the balloon.

blew Linus **blew** the horn.
Linus **made air go** through the horn, and it tooted.

blue

Sally is wearing a **blue** dress. Blue is a **color.** Here is the color blue.

board Linus is carrying a **board.** A board is a **flat piece of wood** cut from a log A board used to be part of a tree.

boat A **boat** carries us over the water. If you want to see a small boat called a **canoe,** look at the picture for the word "beyond." A large boat is called a **ship.**

body Charlie Brown has a strong, healthy **body.** **All the parts of a person or an animal** are its body.

boil When we make water or milk hot enough, it will **boil.** We will see little bubbles on the top of the water, and steam coming from it. One way to **cook** food is to boil it.

bone There is a **bone** on the ground near Snoopy. All dogs like to chew bones. A bone is a hard part of a person or animal's body. If you squeeze your arm, you will feel the bones in your arm.

book Snoopy dreams of writing a **book** some day. He wants to have his picture on the book he writes. The words in a book tell us stories or tell us about things. Some books, like this one, have words and pictures in them. All books have pages fastened together. Some books do not have many pages. This book has a lot of pages.

---

boot

A **boot** is a kind of **shoe.** It covers the foot and a part of the leg. There are several kinds of boots. The boots near Lucy are to wear in the rain or snow, so that her shoes and feet won't get wet and cold.

---

born The tiny kittens were **born** yesterday.
The tiny kittens were **brought into the world** yesterday.

---

borrow I want to **borrow** a book from the library. I will take it home and return it when I have finished reading it.

---

both Linus and Lucy are **both** watching television.
The two of them are watching television.

bother Sometimes when a friend says, "Don't **bother** me," he means, "Please don't **annoy** me." Sometimes when we say, "That bothers me," we mean that it **worries** us.

---

bottle

A **bottle** usually holds things to drink, like milk or juice. Some bottles hold things we must not drink. Do not drink what is in a bottle unless you are sure it is good for you.

---

bottom The lowest part of something is often called the **bottom.**
The floor is the **bottom** of a room.

---

bounce

Lucy is hitting the ball to make it **bounce.**
Lucy is hitting the ball to make it **jump up after it has gone down.**

---

bow Sally is wearing a **bow** in her hair.
In her hair, Sally is wearing a **ribbon that's tied to make two little rings.**

bowl Snoopy eats from a **bowl.**
Snoopy eats from a **deep, round dish.**

box

Linus is pouring breakfast food from a **box.** The box is made of strong, heavy paper, and holds the food. The box has a top and bottom and four sides.

boy A **boy** grows up to become a man. Charlie Brown is a boy. A girl grows up to become a woman. Sally is a girl.

branch

Snoopy is using a **branch** that fell from a tree to toast marshmallows. A branch is a part of a tree.
It grows out of the trunk of the tree.
Leaves grow on the branch of a tree.
Most trees have many branches.

---

bread

Linus is buttering his **bread.** Bread is a **food** made of flour. The flour is formed into a loaf and is baked in an oven.

break "Did you **break** my dish?" asks Peppermint Patty. To break something is to make it come apart in pieces. Snoopy dropped some dishes and they **broke.** They came apart in pieces. The dishes are **broken.**

broke
broken

If you break a rule, you act against the rule.

---

breakfast Sally and Charlie Brown are having **breakfast.** Sally and Charlie Brown are having their **first meal of the day.**

Breakfast is eaten in the morning.

breath Your **breath** is the **air you take in and let out.** When we take air in and let it out, we call it breathing.

breathe When you breathe out in very cold weather, you can see the air. It looks like steam. It must be cold in Charlie Brown's classroom. We can see his breath.

---

breeze A **breeze** is a little wind.

---

brick

Linus is standing near a high **brick** wall. Bricks look like stone blocks, but they are made of clay and are baked in an oven. Bricks are usually red.

---

bridge Snoopy is walking on a little stone **bridge.**
Snoopy is walking on a little **path that crosses the water.** Some bridges support wide roads or even railroad tracks and cross over wide spaces.

---

bright

It's night, and Lucy and Charlie Brown are standing under a **bright** light. Something bright lights up a place.

A **bright** boy learns things easily.

bring Snoopy watches Charlie Brown **bring** him his dinner.
Snoopy watches Charlie Brown **carry** his dinner to him.

brought Charlie Brown **brought** the dish all the way from the kitchen.
He **carried** it from the kitchen.

---

broom Lucy sweeps the floor with a **broom.**
Lucy sweeps the floor with a **brush attached to a long handle.** The handle is called a **broomstick.**

---

brother Linus is Lucy's **brother.** Linus and Lucy have the same mother and father. A boy or a man who has the same parents as you do is your brother.

---

brown **Brown** is a color. This is the color brown

brush Snoopy is busy cleaning the house. On the floor is a **brush.** The hairs of a brush loosen dirt or dust and pick it up. The handle of a brush makes it easy to hold. Some brushes are used for painting.
I use a hair brush to make my hair smooth, and I use a toothbrush to clean my teeth.

---

bubble A **bubble** is a tiny ball of air. I like to make soap bubbles.

---

bug A **bug** is a small **insect.** An **ant** is a bug. Some bugs hop. Some bugs jump.

build Snoopy is planning to **build** a little place to sit, just like Lucy's.
Snoopy is planning to **make** a little place **by putting it together** with wood and other things.

built I wonder who **built** Snoopy's doghouse?
I wonder who **put together** Snoopy's doghouse?

---

bump

Did you see Linus **bump** his head against the table?
Did you see Linus **knock** his head against the table?

Now he may have a **bump** on his head.
Now he may have a **place that hurts** on his head.

---

bunch We put together many flowers to make a **bunch** of flowers.

---

bundle Snoopy is carrying a **bundle** tied to the end of a pole.
A bundle is a **group of things wrapped up together.**

---

bunny **A baby rabbit** is called a **bunny.**

---

burn

You can see that Snoopy's doghouse **is on fire.** You can see it **burn.**

bury Dogs often **bury** bones in the ground You bury something by putting it in a hole in the ground and then covering it over with earth.

bus Charlie Brown missed the school **bus.** A bus works like an automobile, but it is much larger and has seats for many people.

bush Snoopy walks past a **bush.** A bush is a **small tree** with branches and leaves close to the ground.

busy

Charlie Brown is **busy.** He is fixing Snoopy's dinner.
Charlie Brown is **at work.** He is fixing Snoopy's dinner.

but He ran fast, **but** he couldn't catch the dog.
He ran fast, **yet** he couldn't catch the dog.

There is no one in this room **but** you and me.
There is no one in this room **except** for you and me.

---

butcher The **butcher** cuts up meat and sells it. We buy meat from the butcher.

---

butter

Linus is putting **butter** on his bread. Butter is a **food made from cream.**

---

butterfly The **butterfly** seems to enjoy flying around Snoopy. A butterfly is an **insect** with a tiny body and four wings that are much bigger than his body. Butterflies have beautiful wings.

---

button I sewed a **button** on my doll's dress.
I sewed a **small, round fastener** to my doll's dress.

Do you **button** your coat before you go out?
Do you **close** your coat **with its buttons** before you go out?

buy The kids are on line to **buy** tickets to the movies.
To buy something is to **give money and get something for it.**

bought Yesterday I **bought** a pencil for five cents.
Yesterday I **paid** five cents **and got** a pencil.

---

buzz The sound that a bee makes is **"buzz."**

---

by The dog lies **by** the boy.
The dog lies **near** the boy.

I'll be there **by** five o'clock.
I'll be there **no later than** five o'clock.

Violet made the doll dress **by** hand.
Violet made the doll dress **with** her hands.

We sat on the bench **by** the road.
We sat on the bench **at the side of** the road.

cage A **cage** is a **closed place** with wires or bars on the sides. Animals are often kept in **cages.**

cake

Hungry Lucy is about to eat a piece of **cake.** Cake is a **sweet food** made of flour, eggs, milk and sugar, baked in an oven.

calendar A **calendar** shows the days and months of the year.

call Lucy is going to **call** Charlie Brown.
Lucy is going to **telephone** Charlie Brown.

Mother will **call,** "Children, come to lunch."
Mother will **say loudly,** "Children, come to lunch."

My name is Richard, but my friends **call** me Dick.
My name is Richard, but my friends **name** me Dick.

Aunt Elaine came **to call** on us.
Aunt Elaine came **to visit** us.

People who live in the United States of America are **called** Americans.

Didn't you hear me **calling** you? I **called** you three times.

camel The **camel** is an **animal with a big round lump on its back called a hump.** Some camels have two humps.
A man can ride on a camel.

camera

Snoopy is taking a picture of Frieda with his **camera.** Snoopy's camera is a **little box** he uses **for taking pictures.**

camp Charlie Brown and his friends go to **camp** in the summer.
They sleep in tents and play outdoors all day.
Summer camp is fun.

can Charlie Brown is opening a **can** of dog food for Snoopy. A can is **made of metal** and **is used to hold foods** and other things.

I **can** pull myself up.
I **am able** to pull myself up.

cannot Baby **cannot** walk yet.
Baby **is not able** to walk yet.

can't **Can't** means **cannot.** Charlie Brown cannot drive a car yet. He can't drive a car.

could Lucy **could** jump over the rope even though it was very high.
Lucy **was able** to jump over the rope even though it was very high.

couldn't **Couldn't** means **could not.** Sally couldn't jump over the rope.

Canada **Canada** is a country in North America. The United States of America and Canada are neighbors.

candle Linus is carrying a **candle.** A candle is made of wax and a string, and **is used to give us light.** We light candles on a birthday cake—one candle for each year.

---

candy

Lucy is offering you a piece of **candy.** Lucy is offering you **something sweet** to eat.

---

canoe Charlie Brown and Snoopy are in a **canoe.** Charlie Brown and Snoopy are in **a small, light boat.**

cap Linus is wearing a **cap.**
Linus is wearing a **small hat.**

Put a **cap** on the bottle.
Put a **top** on the bottle.

---

captain A **captain** is a **leader.** Charlie Brown is captain of his baseball team. Charlie Brown is the leader of his baseball team.

---

car Charlie Brown has just climbed out of the **car** that brought him home from camp. A car is also called an **automobile.** All cars move on wheels and are used to carry people and things. Railroad cars that are used to carry things are called freight cars.

---

card Charlie Brown is reading a **card** that he got in the mail. A card is a **flat or folded piece** of **stiff paper** that usually has words or pictures on it. There are many kinds of cards. Charlie Brown is reading a birthday card—a card sent to wish him a Happy Birthday. There are picture postcards—cards you can mail when you're visiting places away from home. There are all sorts of playing cards you can use for games.

care Will your mother **care** if you stay and play with me?
Will your mother **worry** if you stay and play with me?
Will it **bother** your mother if you stay and play with me?

I **care** for my kittens.
I **look after** my kittens.

I do not **care** for pie.
I do not **like** pie.

---

careful Lucy is **careful** when she crosses the street. Lucy **pays attention** when she crosses the street. Lucy watches for danger when she crosses the street.

---

careless Roy is **careless** when he crosses the street.
Roy is **not careful** when he crosses the street.

---

carpenter The man who built our house is a **carpenter.** A carpenter puts together the wooden parts of a house, and also makes other things out of wood.

---

carriage Charlie Brown is pushing his little sister in a baby **carriage.** A baby carriage has wheels, and the baby either sits or lies in it. Other carriages are much larger. Kings and queens used to ride in carriages that were pulled by horses.

---

carrot A **carrot** is a **vegetable** that grows in the garden. The part of the carrot we eat is the root. Carrots are orange.

carry

To **carry** something is to **pick it up from one place and take it to another.** Lucy is carrying her sandwich and milk from the kitchen to the television set.
I **carried** the box down the stairs.
Linus carries his blanket with him wherever he goes.

carton Lucy is carrying a **carton** of **milk.** A carton is a **box made of heavy paper.** We put many different kinds of things in cartons.

case A **case** is a **box** that holds many things at once. We put books in a bookcase. We carry clothes in a suitcase.

In case it rains, we will stay home.
If it rains, we will stay home.

castle

Linus is making a **castle** of sand on the beach. A real castle is a large old home with many rooms, built long ago for kings and queens and other rulers. **Castles** were usually built of stone.

---

cat Frieda is carrying a small toy **cat.** A real cat is a small **animal** with fur. My pet is a cat. I call him Harry. A kitten is a baby cat.

---

catch Snoopy can **catch** a ball in his mouth.
Snoopy can **go after and take hold** of a ball in his mouth.

I tried to **catch** my brother.
I **ran after** my brother and tried to get hold of him.

Take off your wet shoes so you won't **catch** a cold.
Take off your wet shoes so you won't **get** a cold.

The cat **catches** mice.

caught The dog **caught** a rabbit. I **caught** a cold.

---

caterpillar A **caterpillar** is a furry **kind of worm.** When it grows, it becomes a butterfly.

cave A **cave** is a big **hole under the ground.** Many animals live in caves.

---

ceiling The inside top part of a room is the **ceiling.**

---

cellar **The room under a house** is the **cellar.** A cellar is sometimes called a **basement.**

---

cent A **cent** is one **penny.** Five cents is equal to a nickel.

---

center The **center** of something is its **middle.**

---

certain Are you **certain** that you closed the door?
Are you **sure** that you closed the door?

Certain foods are not good for me.
I know **some** foods that are not good for me.

---

chain Charlie Brown has Snoopy at the end of a **chain.** Chains are made of metal rings, and bend easily. They are usually stronger and harder to break than rope. We made a paper chain at school with colored paper.

chair Linus is sitting in a comfortable **chair.** A chair is a **seat.** It is something to sit on.

chalk Charlie Brown is holding a piece of **chalk** in his hand. It looks like a **white crayon.** We use chalk for writing on a blackboard.

---

chance There is a **chance** that snow will fall today.
It **may happen** that snow will fall today.

Give me a **chance** to hit the ball.
It is my **turn** to hit the ball.

---

change Lucy gave the grocer a dollar for some eggs. The eggs cost less than a dollar. The grocer gave her **the money that was left** from the dollar. He gave her the **change.**

Do you think the weather will **change?**
Do you think the weather will **become different?**

Mother had to **change** the baby's dress.
Mother had to **take off** what baby was wearing **and put on something else.**

I am going to **change** my doll house furniture.
I am going to **move** my doll house furniture **to different places.**

I **changed** my shoes because they were wet.

---

chase Why does Violet **chase** Charlie Brown?

Why does Violet **run after** Charlie Brown?

The dog **chased** the cat, but the cat ran faster.

---

cheer We gave a **cheer.**
We gave a **happy shout.**

We are **full of cheer.**
We are **happy.**

When our side wins the game, we **cheer.**
When our side wins the game, we **shout happily.**

---

cheerful We are **cheerful** at Christmas time.
We are **merry and full of good cheer** at Christmas time.

Red is a **cheerful** color.
Red is a **bright, gay color.**

cheese **Cheese** is a **food** made of milk. There are many kinds of cheese.

cherry A **cherry** is a small, round **fruit.** Birds like to eat cherries. Cherries grow on trees.

chew

After Linus bites his sandwich, he will **chew** it. We chew with our teeth. We cut food and break it up in our mouths with our teeth. Dogs chew on bones. A baby cannot chew because a baby has no teeth.

chicken A **chicken** is a **bird.** A mother chicken is a **hen** and a father chicken is a **rooster.** The meat of a chicken is good to eat.

chief An Indian **chief** is a **leader** of other Indians.

child A young boy or girl is a **child.** I am the child of my mother and father.

children Boys and girls are **children.** We have three children in our family.

chimney Snoopy is walking past a house that has a **chimney.** The pipe that takes smoke away from a fireplace or stove is called the chimney.

---

chipmunk A **chipmunk** is a small squirrel.

---

chocolate Linus loves **chocolate** candy. Chocolate is made from the same seed used to make cocoa, and is brown.

---

choose Charlie Brown is deciding which Christmas card to **choose.**
Charlie Brown is deciding which Christmas card to **pick out.**

chose Charlie Brown **chose** a green and red card.

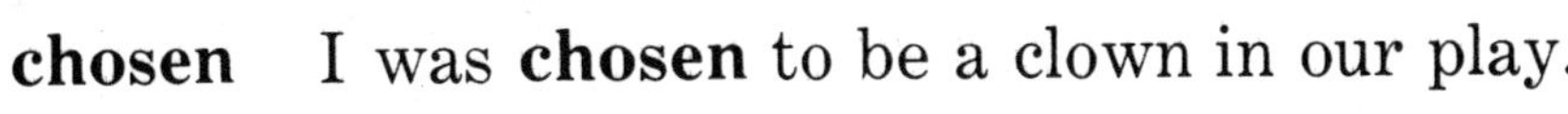

chosen I was **chosen** to be a clown in our play.

Christmas **Christmas** comes every year on December 25. It is the **holiday** on which we remember the day Jesus Christ was born.

---

church A **church** is a place where people come together to think about God.

---

circle A **circle** is shaped like a **ring.** If you drop a stone in the water it makes **circles.** We stand in a circle to play some games.

---

circus A **circus** is a **show.** We usually see it in a tent. The people in the circus can jump, tumble, swing in the air and do other hard tricks. We always see many different animals at the circus.

---

city A **city** is a place where a great many people live and work. In a city you will find many large buildings, schools, apartment houses and factories. There are many cars and buses and trucks in the streets.

---

clap Snoopy began to **clap** and cheer. When we clap, we **hit our hands together** to show that we are pleased. Everyone else **clapped** too.

class

The kids are in the same **class** at school.
The kids are in the same **classroom** with the same teacher, and they learn the same things together.

---

claw The cat scratches with her **claws.**
The cat scratches with the **nails at the ends of her toes.**
Kitty will **claw** me if I tease her.
Kitty will **scratch me with her claws.**

---

clay **Clay** is soft earth used to make bricks and other things.
I can make a bowl out of **clay.**

---

clean Charlie Brown is all **washed** and dressed in **clean** clothes.

Pig-Pen is never **clean.**
Pig-Pen is always covered with dirt and dust.

---

clear The window glass is **clear.**
You can see through the window glass.

The teacher said, "Is that **clear?**"
The teacher said, "Is that **something you understand?**"

The sky is **clear.**
The sun is shining, and there are no clouds in the sky.

climb

Charlie Brown can **climb** over the fence.
Charlie Brown can go up and over the fence by using his hands and feet.

---

clock You look at a **clock** to see what time it is.

---

close I sat **close** to my friend in the room.
I sat **near** my friend in the room.

Please **close** the door.
Please **shut** the door.

I **closed** the book when I finished reading it.

---

closet I hang my clothes in a **closet.**
I hang my clothes in a **small room in which we keep things.**

In my classroom, we have two **closets.**

---

cloth Most of our clothes are made of **cloth.** Silk and cotton are two kinds of cloth.

clothes The things we dress ourselves in are our **clothes.**

cloud 

You can see a white **cloud** in the sky above Snoopy. **Clouds** are made up of tiny drops of water floating close together high in the air.

clown The **funny man** at the circus was the **clown.**

club Snoopy is carrying a golf **club.**
Snoopy is carrying a **stick made of wood,** with a metal end. He uses it to hit a little ball when he plays the game called golf.

A club is a **big and heavy stick.** The giant in stories carries a club.

My mother went to a meeting of her **club.**
My mother went to a meeting of a **group of people.**

coal **Coal** is hard and black, and when it burns it helps make us warm. It is used in furnaces to heat a whole house.

coast The land along the sea or ocean is called the **coast.** It is also called the **seashore.**

I am going to **coast** downhill on a sled.
I am going to **slide** downhill on a sled.

I like **coasting** down the snowy hill.

---

coat Sally is putting on her **coat.**
Sally is putting on **the part of her clothing she wears over her dress and sweater.** Her coat has sleeves to cover her arms.

---

cocoa **Cocoa** is a **hot drink** made of chocolate and milk.

---

coffee My father and mother drink **coffee** for breakfast. Coffee comes from the coffee bean.

---

cold I have a **cold.**
I sneeze and blow my nose, and I feel ill.

Ice cream is **cold.**
Ice cream is **not warm.**

collar

Snoopy's **collar** is made of leather and goes around his neck. The collar of a shirt or dress is the part that fits around the neck.

---

college When I finish high school, I am going to **college.** I am going to a **higher school** where I will learn more things.

---

color Linus is using a crayon to **color** a picture. He is using crayons to add red, blue, yellow and other **colors** to the picture.

Last night I **colored** the pictures in a book.

---

colt A **colt** is a **baby horse.**

---

comb Lucy uses a brush and **comb** to make her hair smooth. First she brushes her hair with a brush. Then she **combs** it with a comb.

When Lucy is finished **combing** her hair, she will tie a ribbon in it.

come To **come** is to move from there to here.

came When I called my dog, he **came** to me.

coming When Mother calls me, I say, "I'm **coming,** Mother."

---

comfortable That big, soft chair is **comfortable.**
That big, soft chair is **good to sit in.** Nothing about that chair bothers me.

---

company Mother is going to have **company** on her trip.
Mother is going to have other people with her, so she won't be alone.

We have **company** at our hose.
We have **people visiting** at our house.

My father works for a big **company.**
My father works for a big **business.**

---

connect Daddy helped me **connect** the parts of my toy railroad.
He helped me **join** them **together.**

---

contain The box can **contain** all my toys.
The box can **hold** all my toys.

A quart of milk **contains** four cups of milk.
A quart of milk **is the same as** four cups of milk.

---

container A **box** is a **container.** It holds things. Bags, bottles, jars and baskets are containers too. They all hold things inside.

cook Snoopy loves to **cook.** Now he is making pancakes. To cook something is to get it ready to eat by heating it.

How are potatoes **cooked?**
Sometimes they are baked in an oven.
Sometimes they are boiled.

I help my mother in the kitchen when she is **cooking.**

---

cookie

A **cookie** is a **small cake.** Lucy is giving cookies to Linus.

---

cool Ice makes water **cool.**
Ice makes water **less warm.**

Mother put the tea in the refrigerator to **cool** it. The cold air in the refrigerator will make the tea less warm.

The day is **cool.**
The day is **not very warm.**

---

copy Woodstock is trying to **copy** Snoopy's trick.
Woodstock is trying to **do the same** trick that Snoopy is doing.

Can you **copy** this picture?
Can you **make** a picture **just like** this one?

corn **Corn** is a grain that is good to eat. Cows and sheep like to eat corn too. Corn grows on large fields that are called cornfields.

---

corner

Linus is standing near the **corner** of a room in the library. The place where two walls meet is called the corner. The place where two streets or roads meet is also called the corner.

---

cost Jack bought a book. It **cost** him fifty cents. The **price** of the book was fifty cents.

---

costume When we dress up in clothes that are not our own, we call it a **costume**. We may wear the costume of a king or clown or Indian chief.

---

cotton **Cotton** is a plant. It is used for making cloth. We use little balls of cotton at home.

---

count Do you **count** the number of times you can jump rope? Lucy **counts** how many times she jumps rope. She **finds out how many** times she jumps rope. She starts with the number one, and then two, and

keeps on counting for as long as she keeps on jumping rope.

He **counted** his pennies.

---

country

Snoopy is walking in the **country.** Snoopy is not walking in the city. He is walking on the **land outside the city** where there are open fields, trees and only small towns.

The United States of America is a **country.** Canada is a country. A whole land and all of its people make up a country.

---

couple Linus has a **couple** of pencils.
Linus has **two** pencils. Two things of the same kind are sometimes called a couple.

---

course Can you spell your name? Of **course** I can.
Can you spell your name? **Surely** I can.

When a ship changes its **course,** it turns and goes another way.

---

cousin My uncle and aunt have two children. The boy is my **cousin** and the girl is my **cousin.** The children of all my aunts and uncles are my **cousins.**

cover Please **cover** the box.
Please **put something over** the box to **close** it.

I **cover** my doll with a blanket.
I **put the blanket over** my doll to keep her warm.

The jar has its own **cover.**
The jar has a **top** which closes it.

We **covered** the seeds with dirt when we planted them.
Hats and hoods are coverings for the head.

---

cow A **cow** is an **animal** that gives us milk. Cows eat grass.

---

cowboy A **cowboy** takes care of cows and other animals. He must know how to ride a horse very well. He has many animals to watch, and often they wander so far apart that the cowboy must ride from one place to another on his horse.

---

crack The cup has a **crack** in it.
The cup has a **small break** in it, but it has not broken into pieces.

We heard a loud **crack** of the gun.
We heard a loud **sound** from the gun.

I like to **crack** nuts.
I like to **break** nuts **open.**

---

cracker A **cracker** is like a cookie but not sweet. Some crackers have salt on them.

cradle A **cradle** is a **small bed for a baby.** Some cradles can rock back and forth.

---

crawl

The baby can **crawl.**
The baby can **move on his hands and knees.**

The baby **crawls** before he learns to walk.

Charlie Brown and Sally are **crawling** on the floor.

---

crayon Linus is choosing a **crayon.** A crayon is like a pencil. You can write and draw and color with it. Crayons come in many different colors. Crayons and candles are both made of wax.

---

cream **Cream** is a part of the milk we get from cows. Sometimes you see cream on the top of the milk. Butter is made from cream.

creep The baby can **creep** on his hands and knees.
The baby can **crawl.**

Sometimes I **creep** up behind my sister and surprise her.
Sometimes I **move slowly and quietly** up to my sister so that she can't hear me, and surprise her.

crept I **crept** up quietly so that she would not hear me.

---

crooked Roy picked up a stick that was **crooked.**
Roy picked up a stick that was **not straight.**

The road was very **crooked.**
The road **had many bends** in it.

---

cross There is a red **cross** on the book Snoopy is reading. When you see a red cross, you know that you can get help in making a sick person better.
You can get help for a person hurt in an accident.

I am **cross** with you.
I am **angry** with you.

Cross the street carefully.
Go from one side of the street **to the other** carefully.

When the sign said "Walk," we **crossed** the street.

crow A **crow** is a **black bird.** Crows eat seeds, and so farmers try to keep crows away from plants.

---

crowd

There's a big **crowd** waiting to play baseball.
There are **many people** waiting to play baseball.

The people **crowd** on to the beach when it's hot.
The people **go** to the beach **in large numbers** when it's hot.

The people **crowded** into the bus.
The store is **crowded** at Christmas time.

---

crumb A **crumb** fell from my piece of cake.
A **small bit** fell from my piece of cake.

In the winter we put bread **crumbs** out for the birds.

---

cry Sally will **cry** if she falls and hurts herself.
Tears will **come** to Sally's eyes if she falls and hurts herself.

When Franklin hurt his finger, he **cried.**

Snoopy got so angry during the baseball game that he started **crying.**

cup

One **cup** on Snoopy's table is lying on its side. We use a cup when we drink hot chocolate because a cup has a handle.

---

cupboard Charlie Brown reaches into the **cupboard** for Snoopy's food. A cupboard is a **small closet with shelves** in which we keep foods, dishes, cups and bowls.

---

curb Charlie Brown sits on the **curb** in front of his house. The curb is the **edge of the sidewalk,** and we step down from the curb into the street.

curl I wind my hair around my finger to make a **curl.** Frieda has many **curls** in her hair.

I like to **curl** up in a chair and look at a book.

curly Frieda is very proud of her **curly** hair. Frieda's hair is **not straight.** Her hair curls into little rings.

---

curtain There is a new blue **curtain** in Linus's room. We hang curtains in front of our windows to make the room look pretty.

---

cut Roy had **a cut** on his finger.
He **cut** his finger with a piece of glass.
He **sliced** it on a piece of glass.

Lucy can **cut** the paper doll.

---

cute My new kitten is **cute.**
My new kitten is **little and pretty.**

D d

Dad I call my father **Dad.** Other names for father are Daddy, Pa, Papa and Pop.

daily The mailman comes to our block **daily.**
The mailman comes to our block **every day.**

daisy Charlie Brown has found a **daisy** growing in the field. "She loves me, she loves me not," says Charlie Brown as he picks the petals off the flower. There are many **daisies** in the field.

dance In the school show, Lucy will **dance.** To dance is to **jump** and turn and **move in time with the music.** Lucy loves **dancing.**

---

dandelion Frieda has picked a **dandelion,** a very bright yellow flower.

---

danger **Danger** means something that can hurt you. If you cross the street without looking, you are in danger of being hit by a car.

dangerous It is **dangerous** to cross the street when cars are coming.
It is **not safe** to cross the street when cars are coming.

---

dare Do you **dare** to climb a tree?
Are you **brave enough** to climb a tree?

---

dark Snoopy is hurrying home because it will soon be night.
The night is **dark.** It's hard to see at night because it is **not light.**

darling **Darling** is what you call someone you love very much.

---

date What **date** is this? The date is November 17. The date on the calendar shows the year, the month, the week and the day.

A **date** is a **fruit.** It grows at the very top of a tall tree.

---

daughter A girl is the **daughter** of her mother and father.

---

day The **day** is the **time when it is light.** It is also called the **daytime.** The night is the time when it is dark. **The daytime and the nighttime together make one day.** There are twenty-four hours in the day. The first day of the week is Sunday. There are seven days in the week.

---

dead The mouse is **dead.** Something that is dead is **not alive.**

December **December** is the twelfth month of the year. It has thirty-one days. Christmas comes in December. In some parts of the country it snows in December.

---

decide Let's **decide** what game we are going to play.
Let's **make up our minds** what game we are going to play.

We **decided** to play baseball.

deed Feeding the birds bread crumbs was a good **deed.**
Feeding the birds bread crumbs was a good **thing to do.**

---

deep

It has rained and rained, and Snoopy's house is **deep** in water.
The bottom of Snoopy's house is covered with water.

A **deep** hole is a hole that has been dug **far into the ground.**

---

deer A **deer** is a **wild animal.** Some deer have horns.

---

deliver Someone has sent Linus a package. Roy **delivers** it to Linus.
Roy **brings** it **to** Linus.

---

den A **den** is a wild animal's home. The squirrel has his den in a hollow tree. The rabbit's den is a hole in the ground.

---

dentist The doctor who fixes your teeth and cleans them is a **dentist.**

desert A **desert** is a dry, sandy piece of land without trees or grass. Very few things grow in the desert because there is so little water there.

---

desk Lucy is sitting at her **desk** reading. Linus is sitting at his desk writing. Charlie Brown isn't working. A desk is a **table on which you read, write or draw.**

---

dessert My favorite dinner is roast beef and potatoes and ice cream for **dessert.**

---

destroy To **destroy** something is to **break it completely.** Snoopy was in such a hurry to eat his dinner that he rushed out of his doghouse and destroyed it. Snoopy broke his doghouse completely.

dew In the early morning there is **dew** on the grass.
In the early morning there are **very small drops of water** on the grass.

---

diamond A **diamond** is a **beautiful stone.** It is as clear as glass and sparkles like a star.

Diamond sometimes means the shape of something, such as the red diamond sign on a playing card.

---

die Flowers **die** when the frost comes.
Flowers **do not live** any longer when the frost comes.

The rat **died** when he was caught in the trap.

---

different Blue and red are **different** colors.
Blue and red are colors that are **not the same.**

Round is **different** from square.

---

dig

Lucy has buried something in the ground. Linus must now **dig** a hole to find what Lucy has hidden there.
Linus must now **make a hole in the ground** if he is to find what Lucy has hidden there.

dug Linus **dug** a deep hole.

---

dime A **dime** is money. A dime buys just as much as two nickels. It buys just as much as **ten cents.** Whenever Charlie Brown gets a dime, he puts it in his dime bank.

dining Peppermint Patty and Marcie are **dining.**
Peppermint Patty and Marcie are **eating.**
They are in a **dining room.**
It is a room used mostly for eating.

---

dinner Charlie Brown eats **dinner** at six o'clock. In his house everyone eats the **main meal of the day** in the evening. Except Snoopy . . . he eats as many times a day as he can.

---

dip The kids **dip** their toes in the water to see how cold it is. Eeek—it's cold! When you put something into a liquid quickly and then take it out again quickly, you **dip** it.

He **dipped** his brush in the paint.

---

dirt Pig-Pen is always covered with **dirt.**
Pig-Pen is always covered with **mud and dust.**

dirty Pig-Pen's hands and face and clothes are **dirty.**
Pig-Pen is **not clean.**

disappear Watch Snoopy **disappear.** One moment he is there—the next moment he is **out of sight.** Now Snoopy is not to be seen. Only his smile has not **disappeared.** His smile remains.

---

dish Peppermint Patty is washing a **dish.** She has a great many **dishes** to wash. There are plates and bowls, cups and saucers. Patty wonders why people have to use so many dishes to eat one meal.

ditch A **ditch** is a long narrow opening dug into the ground to carry off extra water. Sometimes ditches are muddy, but usually they are filled with water and look like little streams.

---

divide When you **divide** a thing you **make it into parts.** It is not whole any more. You can divide an orange between yourself and your friend.

---

do I will **do** all my work today.
I will **start** my work **and finish** it today.

did Lucy said I **did** not see the parade, but I really did.
I really saw the parade.

didn't **Didn't** means **did not.**

does The farmer **does** his work early in the morning.
The farmer works early in the morning.

done My work is **done.**
My work is **finished.**

---

doctor Linus is reading a letter about a little girl who was sick. Her mother took her to the **doctor.** He gave her some medicine to make her well. A doctor is a person who has learned to take care of your health.

dog A **dog** is a tame **animal** kept at home as a **pet.** Snoopy knows many of them.

---

doghouse

Snoopy has a **doghouse.** It is a little house just big enough for a dog. The house protects the dog from rain, snow and cold.

---

doll A **doll** is a **toy** that looks like a person. Baby dolls and little girl dolls are very lifelike. Rag dolls look less real but are soft and fun to play with.

---

dollar A **dollar** is a silver coin or piece of paper **money** used in the United States of America and in some other countries. A dollar will buy as much as one hundred pennies. If bubble gum costs one penny, Charlie Brown and Lucy will have five hundred pieces for their five dollars.

---

donkey A **donkey** is an **animal** that has long ears and looks like a small horse.

door

Charlie Brown was standing in the doorway of the school building when the door shut and made him jump. A **door** shuts or opens the entrance to a room or a building. Closets and cupboards have doors.

---

dot A **dot** is a small round spot like this . A dot at the end of a sentence is called a period. Many dots on a dress are called polka dots.

---

double **Double** means **two** of anything. A double bed is a bed that has room for two people.

When you fold a sheet in two, you **double** it.

When someone says you are a **double** for your father, that means you **look just like him.**

---

dough We use **dough** when we bake. It is made of flour, milk, water, eggs and butter.

down When you go **down,** you go from a higher place to a lower place. Snoopy jumps down from the chair to the floor.

---

downstairs When you start at the top of the stairs and go to the bottom, you are going **downstairs.** Downstairs means the **floor below.**

---

downtown We usually call the busy, crowded part of a city **"downtown."**
People go **downtown** to buy things. Many people work downtown.

---

dozen A **dozen** of anything is **twelve.**

---

dragon A **dragon** is a make-believe animal that was supposed to be very big. He was also supposed to breathe fire.

---

draw Linus decided to **draw** a picture. He made lines with a crayon. To draw means to make a design with a pencil or a pen.
Linus made a **drawing** of Lucy.

drew Linus drew the picture without a mouth because that is the way he would like Lucy best—quiet.

dream The thoughts and pictures that pass through your mind when you are asleep are your **dreams.**

dress Sally and Lucy are each wearing a **dress,** but Peppermint Patty is wearing a shirt and shorts. Girls and women often wear dresses.

dressed Linus is getting **dressed.** Linus is putting on his clothes.

---

drill A **drill** is a **tool** that makes holes in wood or metal.

To drill means to do something over and over until you get it right.

drink

Do you want a **drink** of milk?
Do you want a **glass** of milk?

To **drink** is to **swallow** a liquid like water, milk or root beer.

Snoopy and Lucy are very thirsty. They **drink** their milk. Snoopy **drank** his milk very quickly. Lucy is still **drinking.**

---

drive

Snoopy wants to go for a **drive.**

driver He's pretending that he's the bus **driver,** the **person who drives** the bus.

Snoopy wishes he could really **drive.** He wishes he could **make the bus go** anywhere he chooses.

But he must wait to be **driven.**

Yesterday the bus driver **drove** him to school with the children.

drop Watch out, Charlie Brown, you're about to **drop** all your papers!

Too late—they have all **dropped.** All the papers have **fallen** to the ground.

To drop means to **let fall.**

A **drop** is **a little bit of liquid** that falls like a drop of rain.

---

drown If a person is under water and cannot get air to breathe, he may **drown.**

Then he will be dead.

drum Pig-Pen's musical instrument is a **drum.** It is shaped like a big can. It is hollow and has a kind of skin stretched over it. Pig-Pen plays the drum by beating it with two sticks.

---

dry **Dry** means **not wet.** After we wipe a dish with a towel, it is dry. There is no water left on the dish.

We hang our wash in the sun to **dry.** The hot sun **gets all the water out** of the clothes.

---

duck A **duck** is a **bird** that can swim. A duck can walk too. Wild ducks can fly.

Roy will **duck** if you throw the pillow at him.
Roy will **bend down out of the way** if you throw the pillow at him.

---

during The children played **during** recess.
The children played **as long as** recess lasted.

---

dust The air is full of **tiny pieces of dirt** called **dust.** The dust settles on furniture and floors and makes everything **dusty.**

When Mother **dusts** a table, she wipes away all these tiny bits of dirt and makes the table clean.

E e

each You have a cookie. Your friend has a cookie. **Each** of you has a cookie. Each means **every one of two or more people.**

eagle An **eagle** is a very large **bird.** Ask your father to let you look at a quarter. There is a picture of an eagle on it.

ear An **ear** is what you hear with. Everybody has two **ears,** one on each side of his head. Our ears are small and cup-shaped. Snoopy's long ears hang down except when Charlie Brown shouts at him. Then Snoopy's ears stand straight up.

Ear also means the **handle of a cup or pitcher.**

Sometimes part of a plant is called an ear, such as an **ear of corn.**

early I woke up **early** in the morning.
I woke up when the day was just beginning.

Father came home **early** today.
Father came home before the time he usually arrives.

earn If you cut the grass, you will **earn** twenty-five cents.
If you cut the grass, you will be **paid** twenty-five cents **for your work.**

---

earth The **earth** is what we call **our world.**

Plants grow in the **earth.**
Plants grow in the **soil.**

The **earth** was wet.
The **ground** was wet and soft.

---

east The sun rises in the **east.** If you look at the sun early in the morning, you will be looking east. East is to your right on a map when you read it.

---

easy Something **easy** to do is **not hard** to do. It is easy to jump over a line in the sidewalk. It is not easy to jump over a high fence. When we do something that is easy to do, we say we do it **easily.**

Easter **Easter** is a happy **holiday.** We color eggs at Easter and put them in Easter baskets.

---

eat "Why do I have to **eat** peanut butter every day?" complains Charlie Brown as he takes a bite of his sandwich and chews it.
"I **ate** peanut butter yesterday, and I am **eating** it again today.
I have **eaten** it every day this week. Phooey!"

edge Snoopy is sitting on the **edge** of the roof.
Snoopy is as **close to the end** of the roof **as** he **can be.**

egg Snoopy has found a whole basket full of colored Easter **eggs.** Before someone cooked and colored them, these eggs were brown or white, soft on the inside and hard on the outside. Eggs come from a chicken. They are very good to eat. All birds lay eggs. In some eggs baby birds grow until they are ready to be born.

eight **Eight** is a number that looks like this 8. Let's count to eight: 1 2 3 4 5 6 7 8.

either I have two kittens. You may have **either** of them.
You may have **one or the other** of them.

elbow Charlie Brown has hurt his **elbow.** The elbow is between the upper and lower parts of the arm. The elbow is the place where the arm bends.

electric Anything that needs electricity to work is called **electric.** Your house has electric lights. Your mother has an electric iron. **Electricity** makes lamps light and makes television sets work.

elephant An **elephant** is the largest four-legged **animal** in the world. It has a long nose, called a trunk. It has big ears. Elephants are very strong.

---

eleven **Eleven** is a number that looks like this **11.** Let's count to eleven: 1 2 3 4 5 6 7 8 9 10 **11.**

---

else Who **else** is going?
What **other person** is going?

What **else** would you like to eat?
What **other thing** would you like to eat?

Let's go some place **else.**
Let's go to some **different** place.

---

empty Snoopy has a bunch of **empty** bottles.
Snoopy has a bunch of bottles with **nothing in them.**

emptied The bottles used to be full of juice, but now every bottle has been **emptied**.

---

end The teacher holds the stick by one **end.** She points the other end at the map.

Let's stay until the **end** of the show.
Let's stay until the show is **finished.**

---

engine An **engine** is a machine that makes something work. An automobile engine uses gas to make the car go.

engineer An **engineer** is the **person who runs the engine.**

---

enjoy When you **enjoy** a thing, you like it, and it makes you feel happy. Children enjoy picnics. Grownups enjoy picnics too.

We **enjoyed** seeing the clown do tricks at the circus.

---

enough I have **enough** money to go to the show.
I have **as much** money **as is needed** to go to the show.

---

enter You **enter** the house through the door.
You **go into** the house through the door.

---

envelope Charlie Brown wrote a letter and put it in an **envelope.** Charlie Brown wrote a letter and put it in a **folded piece of paper** with **glue** on the back. On the front of the envelope he wrote the name and address of the person to whom he was sending the letter, and he put a stamp in the corner.

---

equal Lucy and Frieda are of **equal** weight.
Lucy and Frieda are the **same** weight.

Five cents is **equal** to a nickel.
Five cents is the **same as** a nickel.

This sign = means **is equal to.** 2 + 2 = 4.

escape I keep my rabbit inside a fence so he won't **escape.**
I keep my rabbit inside a fence so he won't **get away.**

Eskimo An **Eskimo** is a person who lives in the far north, where it is very cold. There is much ice and snow in the land of the Eskimos.

---

even

Snoopy is resting after a hard game. The game was **even.** Nobody won. Each team was as good as the other.

How can Snoopy lie on a roof that isn't **even?**
How can Snoopy lie on a roof that isn't **level** and isn't **flat?**

The top of Frieda's head is **even** with the top of Snoopy's house. Frieda's head and the roof are the **same** height.

---

evening The **evening** is the time between sunset and nighttime.

---

ever Have you **ever** seen the cow jump over the moon?
Have you **at any time** seen the cow jump over the moon?

---

every The farmer gave **every** boy an apple.
The farmer gave **each** boy an apple.

Every apple the farmer had was gone.
All the farmer's apples were gone.

everybody Charlie Brown is trying to listen to **everybody.**
Charlie Brown is trying to hear what **each person** has to say.

everyone **Everyone** has something to say.
Each person has something to say.

everything Outdoors, **everything** is covered with snow.
Each thing that is outside is covered with snow.

everywhere The snow is **everywhere.**
The snow is **every place** you look. There is snow **all over** the ground.

exact The **exact** price of this doll is one dollar.
The price of this doll is not a penny more nor a penny less than one dollar.

exactly It is **exactly** five o'clock.
It is not earlier nor later than five o'clock.
It is **just** five o'clock.

---

except All the children **except** Charlie Brown are on the bus.
All the children **but** Charlie Brown are on the bus.

excuse Charlie Brown's **excuse** for being late was that his alarm clock didn't work.
The **reason** Charlie Brown gave for being late was that his alarm clock didn't work.

He asked the teacher to **excuse** him for being late.
He asked the teacher to **pardon** him for being late.

His mother **excused** him from the table.
His mother **said he could leave** the table.

---

expect We **expect** to get a letter today.
We **think** we shall get a letter today.

---

explain I will **explain** how to use the radio.
I will **make you understand** how to use the radio by telling you.

I will **explain** the puzzle.
I will **make you understand** the puzzle by showing you.

---

eye Sally is covering her **eye** with her hand. Charlie Brown wants to find out how well she sees.
Our eyes are what we see with.
Everybody has two eyes.

Ff

face The front part of your head is your **face.** Your eyes, your nose, your cheeks and your mouth are parts of your face.

Charlie Brown and Linus are **face to face.**
The front part of Charlie Brown's head and the front part of Linus's head are turned toward each other.

fact A **fact** is a thing that is true. It is a fact that the world is round. This book tells you many facts.

factory A **factory** is a **building** where something is made. Automobiles are made in a factory. Airplanes are made in a factory.

fail When you try to catch a ball and you miss, you **fail** to catch the ball.

If Charlie Brown does not work harder at school, he will **fail.**
If Charlie Brown does not work harder at school, he **will not pass** on to the next grade. He will not succeed in finishing the work for his grade.

fair A **fair** is so full of things to see and do that Charlie Brown and Peppermint Patty don't know where to begin. There are rides and games and many shows. There are prize animals to see and prize foods to taste. No wonder everyone loves a fair.

The day is **fair.**
The day is **warm and sunny.**

Charlie Brown and Patty shared their food. They thought that was **fair.**
They thought that was the **right thing to do.**

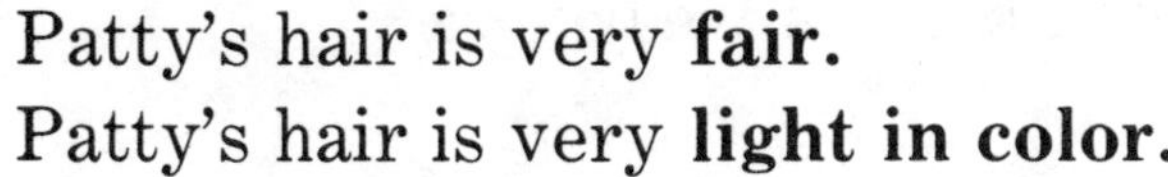

Patty's hair is very **fair.**
Patty's hair is very **light in color.**

Everyone likes to play with Linus because he is **fair.**
Everyone likes to play with Linus because he is **honest.**

fairest Who is the **fairest** in the land?
Who is the **prettiest** in the land?

---

fairy A **fairy** is not a real person. **Fairies** are storybook creatures who are very tiny and can do magic things.

---

fall Snoopy has had a bad **fall.** He has dropped from a high branch down to the ground. He has **fallen** on his head. He **fell** because he climbed too high.

Fall is the season of the year that follows summer. The leaves of some trees change color in the fall. Another word for fall is **autumn.**

false The leader of this Halloween band is wearing a **false** face.
The leader of this Halloween band is wearing a **make-believe** face. It is not his real face. It is a mask.

A **false** story is one that is **not true.**

---

family Charlie Brown has a mother and a father and a baby sister. They are his **family.**

---

fan A **fan** is used to move the air and make you feel cool. Some fans are made of paper and are held in your hand.
You **fan** yourself by waving one back and forth in front of you.

Electric **fans** have blades, like big petals, that go round and round to make a breeze.

---

fancy Sally's new dress is **fancy.**
Sally's new dress is **not plain.** It has much trimming on it.

far The hills are **far** away.
The hills are **not near.**

How **far** is it to your school?
Is is **a long way or a short way** to your school?

My old shoes are **far** too small for me.
My old shoes are **much** too small for me.

---

fare I had to pay a **fare** on the bus.
I had to pay **money** to ride on the bus.

---

farm A **farm** is a piece of land where food is grown and animals are raised. On most farms you will see horses, stables and barns, and fields and pastures.

---

farmer The **person** who owns a farm or works on a farm is called the **farmer.**

---

farther The red house is **farther** away than the yellow one.
The red house is a **greater distance from** here than the yellow one.

---

fast Linus can skate very **fast.**
Linus can skate very **quickly.**

Snoopy can run **faster** than Lucy.
Snoopy can get from one place to another **in a shorter time** than Lucy.

Snoopy is the **fastest** runner of all.
Snoopy is the **swiftest** on his feet.

fasten Make sure you **fasten** the door.
Make sure you **close** the door tightly.
Make sure the door is **fastened.**

Mother **fastened** a button to the jacket.
Mother **sewed** a button to the jacket.

fastener A button that keeps your clothes closed is called a **fastener.**

---

fat If Snoopy were to eat everything he wanted, he would be **fat.**
If Snoopy were to eat everything he wanted, he would **not** be **thin.**

Mother uses **fat** for cooking. Mother cooks things in **oil.**

---

father Your **father** is married to your mother.

---

faucet The thing on the sink that turns the water on and off is a **faucet.**

---

fault Whose **fault** is it that the dish was broken?
Who is to **blame** for breaking the dish?

---

fear

Linus feels **fear** when Lucy shouts at him.
Linus is **afraid** when Lucy shouts at him.

---

feast The Thanksgiving table was covered with a **feast.**
The Thanksgiving table was covered with a **big and fancy dinner.**

---

feather Sally is wearing an Indian **feather** hat.
It's big but very light and soft.
Feathers are the **covering of birds.**

February **February** is the second month of the year. February has twenty-eight days. Every fourth year, February has twenty-nine days.

---

feed

Charlie Brown is about to **feed** Snoopy.
Charlie Brown is about to **give** Snoopy his **food.** He is feeding him two dinners at once.

---

feel Patty can **feel** the rain.
Patty can **touch** the drops of rain that are falling. She touched the grass, and **felt** the raindrops on the grass.

The rain gives her a happy **feeling.**
The rain makes her happy.

---

feet On your **feet,** Charlie Brown! Everybody has two feet—a left foot and a right foot. We walk by stepping forward first with one foot, then with the other.
Most animals have four feet.

We measure things by **feet** and inches. One foot is twelve inches long. Charlie Brown is three feet tall. He measures thirty-six inches from his feet to the top of his head.

---

fellow He is a jolly good **fellow.**
He is a jolly good **man.**

---

female A **female** is a girl or a woman. Mother is a female. Father is a male.

fence There is a **fence** around the school yard. Charlie Brown is outside this wire **wall.** He cannot get into the school yard because he cannot climb over the fence. Some fences are made of wooden posts.

---

few There are **few** cars on this road.
There are **not many** cars on this road.

field What kind of **field** is Snoopy in?
It is not a cornfield because there is no corn growing. It is not a wheat field because there is no wheat. Only grass and flowers are growing on this field. A field is a **flat piece of land.** It is sometimes called a **meadow.** Snoopy is pretending he is on a field at an airport, where airplanes land and take off.

---

fierce The **fierce** lion roared.
The **wild** lion roared.

---

fifteen The number **fifteen** looks like this: **15.** Let's count to fifteen:
1 2 3 4 5 6 7 8 9 10 11 12 13 14 **15.**

---

fifth Thursday is the **fifth** day of the week. There are four days before Thursday.

---

fifty The number **fifty** looks like this: **50.**

Half a dollar is **fifty** cents.
Half a dollar is **50** cents.

---

fight Violet and Lucy are having a **fight.** They are angry with each other. They do not hit with their hands. They are **fighting** with words. They shout and say mean things to each other. When they agree again, they will be sorry they **fought.**

fill I will **fill** the basket with cherries. Then it will hold no more. It will be **full.** It will have all it can hold.

Father **filled** the car with gasoline.
Now he is **filling** the pail with water.

---

final We took one **final** look at the lake before we left for home. We took one **last** look at the lake.

---

finally Snoopy had been gone two days. **Finally** he came home. **At last** he came home.

---

find Linus is trying to **find** something in the grass. What does he hope to **see?**

found Good—he has **found** what he was looking for. He **came upon** it by chance.

---

fine It is a **fine** day.
It is a **sunny, bright** day.

You're looking **fine.**
You're looking **well.**

A spider's web is made of **fine** threads.
A spider's web is made of **thin** threads.

Daddy will have to pay a **fine** for parking in the wrong place.
Daddy will have to pay **money** for parking in the wrong place.

---

finger

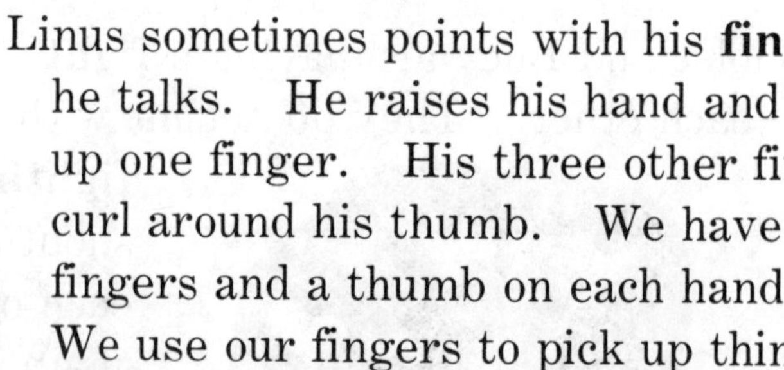

Linus sometimes points with his **finger** when he talks. He raises his hand and holds up one finger. His three other fingers curl around his thumb. We have four fingers and a thumb on each hand. We use our fingers to pick up things. Most animals do not have fingers. They have toes.

fingernail A **fingernail** is a hard little cover on the end of each finger that protects the finger.

---

finish We will **finish** our work very soon.
We will **come to the end** of our work very soon.

Mother **finished** sewing my dress.

fire Charlie Brown loves marshmallows toasted over a **fire.** A fire can do good things. A fire cooks food and makes us warm. It burns with a beautiful, bright light. A fire can do bad things too. It can burn down houses and buildings if people are not careful with it. Fire will burn you if you touch it.

---

fireman A **fireman** protects us from bad fires. He is the **man who puts the fires out.**

---

fire truck Firemen ride on a **fire truck.** The fire truck carries water and hoses and everything the firemen need to put out a fire. A fire truck is also called a **fire engine.**

---

fireplace In our house, we make fires in a **fireplace.** The smoke and flame go up the chimney.

---

first

Charlie Brown is **first** in line.
There is no one in front of Charlie Brown.
One is the **first** number.
There are no numbers before one.

fish Charlie Brown is trying to catch a **fish.** A fish is an **animal that lives in the water.** The fish waves its tail to help it swim around. Most fish are good to eat.

---

fit Father wants a hat to **fit** his head.
Father wants a hat that is **the right size** for his head.

Sally has grown so big that her dress won't **fit** her.
Sally has grown so big that her dress is no longer **the right size** for her.

---

five **Five** is a number that looks like this: **5.** Let's count to five: 1 2 3 4 **5.**

---

fix I broke my toy. Daddy will **fix** it.
Daddy will **put it together again.** Daddy will make it work right again.

---

flag Snoopy is carrying the **flag** of his favorite school. It is a **piece of cloth** with colors and letters on it, chosen by the school. The colors of the flag of the United States of America are red, white and blue. The flag is the **sign** of the country. The Canadian flag is red and white and has a picture of a leaf.

flame The light you see when a fire burns is the **flame.** Flames are red and yellow and orange.

---

flash When we see a light go on and off quickly, we see a **flash** of light.

Lightning **flashes** when there is a storm.

---

flat Snoopy is lying **flat** on his back. He is spread out on his roof. His back is not bent. He is not standing up. He is lying across the roof with his back **straight and even.**

---

float Linus and Sally watch the balloon **float** through the air. The balloon is slowly flying up to the sky. No one is holding the balloon up. The wind carries it. It floats.

A boat will **float** on water.
A boat will **stay on top of the water.** It will **not sink.**

flock A group of animals that live and travel together is a **flock.**

There goes a **flock** of birds. There goes a flock of sheep.

My hens **flocked** into the barnyard.
My hens **moved together** into the barnyard.

---

floor Lucy is sitting on the **floor** watching television. She is sitting on the **bottom part of the room.** Linus is standing behind her. His feet are also on the bottom part of the room.

The room they are in is on the ground **floor** of the house. It is on the first floor. Their bedrooms are on the second floor. Their bedrooms are upstairs.

---

flour Wheat and other grains are rubbed into very small pieces. This **powder made from the wheat** is called **flour.** Mother uses flour to make cakes and bread.

---

flower A **flower** is the pretty **part of a plant.** It has petals and is brightly colored. Roses are red flowers. Violets are blue flowers. Girls and bees like them.

fly Woodstock does not **fly** very well.
He makes his wings go up and down and he moves through the air, but he does not get very high. He only **flies** a little way off the ground.

flew Yesterday a flock of birds **flew** by. They were **flying** south.

flown By December, most birds have **flown** south for the winter.

Can you **fly** a plane?
Can you **pilot** a plane?

A **fly** landed in the soup.
A **small insect** with wings flew into the soup.

---

fold To **fold** a sheet of paper, **bend** one half over the other.

---

follow Charlie Brown wants to **follow** Linus.
Charlie Brown wants to **walk behind** Linus. He prefers Linus to go first so he can **come after.**

food Here comes your **food,** Snoopy! Food is what we eat. Horses eat hay for their food. Grass is food for cows. Snoopy likes the food that people eat—meat, vegetables, milk and bread. What kind of food do you like best?

---

fool Charlie Brown acted like a **fool.**
Charlie Brown acted like a **silly person.** He did not use good sense. He tried to **fool** the baby. He pretended he was a bear. But the baby was not **fooled.** She knew who was growling at her.

---

foot Charlie Brown has one **foot** on the bench. He is standing on his other foot. Linus is walking on both feet. Your foot is at the bottom of your leg.

The blanket is at the **foot** of the bed.
The blanket is at the **end farthest** from the pillow.

The ball rolled to the **foot** of the hill.
The ball rolled to the **base** of the hill.

This ruler is one **foot** long.
This ruler measures **twelve inches.**

---

football Charlie Brown is running and carrying a **football.** The football is made of leather so it is strong enough to be carried, kicked or thrown. In a **football game,** two teams have the chance to carry, throw or kick the football to the end of a field. In a real football game, there are eleven players on each team.

for We used a sheet **for** a curtain at our show.
We used a sheet **in place of** a curtain at our show.

Mother came **for** me.
Mother came **to get** me.

Sally is dressed **for** a party.
Sally is dressed **to go to** a party.

I asked for a bicycle **for** my birthday.
I asked to get a bicycle **as a** birthday present.

When I grow up, I'm going to work **for my father.**
When I grow up, I'm going to work **in my father's office.**

How much did you pay **for** your candy?
How much did you pay **to buy** your candy?

---

forest A **forest** is a **large woods** with many trees. We walked on a path that went through the forest.

---

forget Did you **forget** my books?
Did you **not remember** my books?

Did you forget your new teacher's name? You must try to keep it in mind.

forgot Mary **forgot** her doll.

forgotten I have **forgotten** where I left my cap.

---

fork We eat with a **fork.** We use a knife to cut our food and a fork to lift it to our mouth.

forward Walk **forward.**
Walk **ahead.**

You can walk backward, but it is easier to walk **forward.**

---

fountain Charlie Brown likes to drink from a water **fountain.**

Water sprays from a fountain. The water comes out in a little stream — oops, it may hit Charlie Brown in the face. There is a big and pretty fountain downtown. It shoots water up into the air. Then the water falls into a little pool.

---

fourth D is the **fourth** letter in the alphabet.
A is first.
B is second.
C is third.
D is **fourth.**

---

free The water in the drinking fountain is **free.**
The water in the drinking fountain **costs nothing.**

The people in the United States of America are **free.**
The people in the United States of America can **live as they please.**

---

freeze Snoopy has been waiting all winter for the lake to **freeze.** He has been waiting for the weather to get cold enough to **turn the water to ice.** It **froze** during the night. Now that the lake is **frozen,** he can skate on it.

froze

frozen

freight The **freight** is the **load** of things the freight train carries. If the train carries oranges and machines, then they are the freight.

---

fresh The vegetables are **fresh.**
We **just picked** the vegetables from the garden.

I will get a **fresh** piece of paper.
I will get a piece of paper that has **never been used.**

When we open the window, **fresh** air comes in.
When we open the window, the air that comes in is **clean and cool.**

Sometimes Lucy gets **fresh.**
Sometimes Lucy **answers back in a mean way.**

---

friend Snoopy is Charlie Brown's **friend,** and Charlie Brown is Snoopy's friend. A friend is **someone who likes you.** They like each other very much and always tell each other the truth. They like to be together and help each other.

frog A **frog** is a **small green animal** that can live on land or in the water. A frog jumps from place to place on its strong back legs.

---

from Lucy is tired **from** jumping rope.
Lucy is tired **because** she jumped rope so long.

I took a penny **from** my pocket.
I took a penny **out of** my pocket.

Our house is a long way **from** the school.
The school and our house are a long way **apart.**

We got a letter **from** my aunt today.
We got a letter **sent by** my aunt today.

---

front Snoopy is sitting in **front** of the bakery.
Snoopy is sitting **before** the bakery.

The **front** of the store has a big window.

The door of the store is at the **front** of the store.

frost The **frost** is frozen dew. On a very cold morning, the trees and plants are covered with frost. Inside our home, there is often frost on the windows. The water in the air freezes on the cold windows. We can draw pictures in the frost.

---

fruit An orange is one kind of **fruit.** Apples, peaches and bananas are fruits too. Most fruits grow on trees. Some fruits, like grapes and watermelons, grow on vines.

---

full Lucy's basket if **full.** There is no more room in it for anything else. It cannot hold any more.

---

fun The children are having **fun.**
The children are having **a good time.**

---

funny Snoopy is **funny.**
Snoopy **makes people laugh.**

fur The skin of many animals is covered with **thick, soft hair** that is called **fur.** A cat has fur. A bear has fur.

furry My cat is soft and **furry.**

---

furnace Our home is heated with a **furnace.**
Our home is heated with **a big stove.** We burn coal in our furnace. In some furnaces they burn oil. The furnace is usually in the basement of a house or building.

---

furniture In the house where Lucy and Linus live, there are tables and chairs. That is their **furniture.** Beds and desks are furniture too.

Gg

gallon There are **four quarts** in a **gallon.** We took a gallon of lemonade to the picnic.

gallop Have you ever seen a horse **gallop?**
Have you ever seen a horse **run** as fast as it can?

game

Charlie Brown and his friends are playing a **game** of ball.
A game is played for fun.
Every game has its own rules.

garden A **garden** is a **piece of land** in which plants are grown. Linus grows pumpkins and flowers in his garden.

gas The stove in our kitchen burns **gas.** Our meals are cooked on a gas stove. Some people have electric stoves.

Gas is also a short word for **gasoline.**

gate A **gate** is a **short door,** usually found outdoors in fences or walls.

---

gather Mother will **gather** the children and take them home.
Mother will **bring** the children **together** and take them home.

---

gay

Snoopy is **gay.**
Snoopy is **happy.**

---

gentle Linus is very **gentle.**
Linus is very **kind and nice.**

gently He gives Woodstock a gentle pat.
He gives Woodstock a soft, light pat.
He pats him **gently.**

---

get Please **get** the book for me.
Please **pick up** the book and bring it to me.

I will **get** to school on time.
I will **reach** school on time.

If you play hard, you **get** tired.
If you play hard, you **become** tired.

Linus has been **getting** better grades at school

got I got a cold because I got my feet wet.

---

giant In my storybook there's a story about a **giant.** Giants are make-believe people who were supposed to be **very big** and very strong. When a real man is very big, he is sometimes called a giant.

---

gift Pig-Pen and Charlie Brown each have a **gift** for Violet.

Pig-Pen and Charlie Brown each have a **present** for Violet. Something you give someone at special times—such as Christmas or a birthday—is a gift.

---

giraffe The **giraffe** is an **animal** with very long legs and a very long neck. His neck is so long that he can eat the leaves from tree branches.

---

girl Sally Brown is a little **girl.** A girl grows up to become a woman.

give

When you **give** something to someone, you let her have it to keep. It's fun to give presents.

I **give** you my pencil.
You **may keep** my pencil. You don't have to pay me for it.

Pig-Pen is **giving** a present to Violet.
Charlie Brown **gave** her a present too.

Violet was **given** many presents for her birthday.

---

glad Snoopy is **glad** to go skating.
Snoopy is **happy** to go skating.

---

glass A **glass** is used for drinking. Snoopy likes to drink from a glass because the glass is clear and he can see what's in it. Snoopy drank two glasses of juice.

The windows are made of **glass.** Glass is clear and hard. It keeps out the rain, the wind and the cold weather.

glasses

Glasses is a short word for **eyeglasses.** Snoopy wears glasses because they help him see better.

---

glove A **glove** is a covering for the hand. Gloves are usually made of leather or wool. Gloves have a separate place for each finger. Mittens are like gloves but have one place for the fingers and a separate place for the thumb.

---

glue We use **glue** to **stick** things **together.** I will glue the leg back on my doll's chair.

---

go To **go** is to **move from one place to another.** Sally and Charlie Brown's father wants to drive them to school, but his car won't go. It won't **run.** It won't **move.**

This street doesn't **go** to school.
This street doesn't **lead** to school.

Where do these books **go?**
Where do these books **belong?**

Let's **go** swimming.
Let's **take** a swim.

How does that song **go?**
How does that song **sound?**

Don't **go** to any trouble.
Don't **put yourself** to any trouble.

That skirt doesn't **go** with this sweater.
That skirt doesn't **look nice** with this sweater.

goes Some days nothing **goes** right.
Some days nothing **happens** right.

The light is **going.**
The light is **disappearing.**

gone Soon it will be **gone.**
Soon there will be **none left.**

---

goat A **goat** is an **animal** with horns on its head and a little beard.

---

gobble The sound a turkey makes is **"Gobble, gobble."**

Mother says, "Don't **gobble** your food."
Mother says, "Don't **eat** your food **too fast."**

God We pray to **God** because we feel He loves us and takes care of us. We learn that God made the world and all its people, animals and plants.

---

gold **Gold** is a shiny yellow **metal.** Daddy has a gold watch. Mother has a pin made of gold.

goldfish A **goldfish** is a small, pretty **fish** that is orange. We have a goldfish that lives in a fish bowl and swims around all day long.

---

golf Snoopy is playing **golf.** Golf is a **game** that is played with a small white ball and a set of clubs. Snoopy's friend hit the ball with his club and sent it across the grass into a small hole in the ground. Now Snoopy must try to do the same thing.

Snoopy is unhappy. He tried ten times before the ball went in the hole. His friend hit the ball only twice to make it go in the hole. So Snoopy is losing the game.

---

good Patty is a **good** girl.
Patty does **kind** things. She does not act in bad or mean ways.

Milk is **good** for you.
Milk **helps you grow and be strong.**

When we say that something tastes **good,** we mean that we **like the way it tastes.**

"I feel **good,**" says Peppermint Patty. She means that she feels **happy and healthy.**

goodbye The children waved **goodbye.**
The children waved when they went away.

---

good morning When I get up, Mother says, **"Good morning."**

---

good night When I go to bed at night, Mother says, **"Good night."**

---

goose The **goose** is a bird that looks like a large duck. The other **geese** have just come out.

---

grade I am in the second **grade** in school.
I am in the second **year** in school.

I got a good **grade** on my paper.
I got a good **mark** on my paper. It showed I knew the answers to the teacher's question.

---

grain The farmer grows **grain.** Wheat and oats are different kinds of grain. One **seed** of wheat is also called a grain. See the tiny grain in the farmer's hand.

---

grand Our library is a **grand** building.
Our library is a **large and beautiful** building.

grandfather Your father's father is your **grandfather.**
Your mother's father is your grandfather too.

---

grandma **Grandma** is a pet name for **grandmother.**

---

grandmother Your father's mother is your **grandmother.**
Your mother's mother is your grandmother too.

---

grandpa **Grandpa** is a pet name for **grandfather.**

---

grape A **grape** is a small round **fruit** that grows in bunches.
Mother puts a bunch of grapes into the dish.

---

grapefruit A **grapefruit** is a round yellow **fruit.** It is bigger than an orange and grows on trees.

---

grass **Grass** is a green **plant** that grows in the ground. Snoopy likes to lie on the grass, but he doesn't like to cut the grass.

grasshopper A **grasshopper** is a **bug** that can jump high.

---

gray **Gray** is a **color** made by mixing black and white. This is the color gray.

---

great George Washington was a **great** man.
George Washington was a **very smart and important man.**

The elephant is a **great** animal.
The elephant is a **very big** animal.

Linus says the **Great** Pumpkin is very **important.** Linus always hopes to see the Great Pumpkin at Halloween.

---

green The grass behind Snoopy and Lucy is **green.** This is the color green

Plants are green. The leaves of some trees are green.

When we mix the colors yellow and blue, we get green.

ground

Linus is digging a hole in the **ground.** He is digging the **earth** beneath him. Charlie Brown is standing on the ground behind him.

---

group Meet the Peanuts **group.**

This group is almost always together.
This **bunch** of kids is almost always together. They play together. **Several people together** are a group.

Starting on the left is Woodstock. Then you see Schroeder, Roy, Snoopy, Charlie Brown, Patty, Lucy, Frieda, Linus and Sally.

---

grow Plants, animals and people **grow.**
Plants, animals and people **get larger.** A little plant can grow to become a big plant. A kitten can grow to become a cat. A boy can grow to become a man. Sally grows fast because she eats food that is good for her.

It is spring. All the trees and plants are **growing.**

grew The little colt **grew** until he was a beautiful horse.

---

growl If Lucy makes Snoopy angry, he will **growl.**
He will make a low rumbling sound and roar it out.
When a dog growls, be careful.

---

grown-up My father is a **grown-up.**
My mother is a **grown-up.**
I am **growing up** now, and when I have many more birthdays, I will be a **grown-up.**

---

guard Who is the **guard** protecting Charlie Brown's house?

Who is the person watching over Charlie Brown's house?
Is it a policeman?
No, Snoopy is **guarding** Charlie Brown from harm.

guess I said the stone was in Roy's left hand. I made a good **guess.** I was right.

Lucy must **guess** the answer to the riddle.
Lucy must **try to think of** the answer to the ridde.

---

guest

Pig-Pen is Violet's **guest.** Pig-Pen is visiting Violet at her home. Charlie Brown is another guest. He is also a **visitor.**

---

guide A **guide** is a **person who shows people the way.**
Will you **guide** me through the woods?
Will you **show me the way** through the woods?

---

gum Chewing **gum** is made in flat, thin sticks. We chew gum, but we don't swallow it. It tastes good.

---

gun Snoopy has a toy **gun.** It won't shoot anybody. It can't be used to hurt people.

Hh

ha When Linus laughs, he says, **"Ha, ha!"**

hair Schroeder has light **hair.** Lucy has black hair. Hair covers our heads. The hair that covers animals is called fur.

half Lucy cut the apple in **half.**
Lucy cut the apple in two parts, each the same size.

hall The front room in our apartment is the **hall.** It leads to the other rooms.

Halloween **Halloween** is the last night in October. On this **holiday** some children wear masks like Charlie Brown's. Others wear funny clothes like Lucy's. The kids come to the door and say, "Trick or treat." If they don't get a treat like a candy, they will play a trick on the people who didn't give them something good to eat. Now most kids gather money on Halloween for poor children all over the world.

---

hammer There goes Snoopy with his wood and his **hammer.**

A hammer is a **tool** with a wooden handle and a metal head.

Snoopy **hammers** nails into wood.
Snoopy **hits nails with his hammer** until they are pushed all the way into the wood.

A hammer pounds nails into wood.

hand "Which **hand** hurts?" asks Lucy. The hand is the part of our body with which we hold things. It is just below the wrist at the end of our arm. We have five fingers on each hand.

Please **hand** me the book.
Please **use your hand to give** me the book.

A clock has **hands.** One hand points to the hour and the other hand points to the minute.

---

handkerchief I carry a **handkerchief** in my pocket. It is made of cotton cloth. I blow my nose in it.

---

handle Lucy holds the shovel by its **handle.** The handle of something is the **part we hold in our hand** when we use it. A hammer has a handle. A glass usually does not.

Please **handle** that plate carefully.
Please **hold** that plate carefully.

hang

How did that happen, Charlie Brown? It's not unusual to see a kite **hang** from a tree, but we don't often see a boy hang from a tree upside down. To hang is **to be held from above.** Charlie Brown is being **held** from above by the kite string

Charlie Brown and the kite are **hanging** from the tree.

held
hung

The coat **hangs** on the hook. The coat is **held** up by the hook. We **hung** our coats in the closet.

---

hanger We use a **hanger** when we hang our clothes in a closet. Most hangers are made of strong wire. Some hangers are made of wood.

---

happen When did the accident **happen?**
When did the accident **take place?**

We **happened** to meet at the store.
We **met by chance** at the store.

happy Lucy is so **happy,** she is jumping for joy. When you are happy, you are **very pleased and very glad.** You smile and feel good.

Lucy is **happier** than Sally.
Lucy is **gladder** than Sally.

Lucy is the **happiest** girl in the bunch.
Lucy is the **most pleased** girl in the bunch.

---

hard The rock is **hard.** You can't press it or change its shape. The pillow is soft. You can press it and change its shape.

That was a **hard** thing to do.
That was **not** an **easy** thing to do.

hardly We **hardly** had time to eat our dinner.
We **only just** had enough time to eat our dinner.

---

harm Sally will not **harm** the butterfly.
Sally will not **hurt** the butterfly.

hat

Woodstock says, "Do you like my new **hat,** Snoopy?" A hat is a **covering worn on the head.**

hatch The hen will **hatch** the eggs by sitting on them.
The hen will make the baby birds inside the eggs ready to be born by sitting on the eggs and keeping them warm.

hate Lucy wants Schroeder to pay more attention to her and less to playing his piano. "I **hate** your piano," she says. To hate something is to **dislike it very much.** Lucy hates the piano so much she kicks it and almost breaks it.

have "Woodstock, you **have** a ball in your mouth."
"Woodstock, you **are holding** a ball in your mouth."

"You will **have** to drop the ball."
"You **must** drop the ball."

Woodstock **has** a ball.
Woodstock **is holding** a ball.

Woodstock **had** a ball. He doesn't have one anymore. Now Snoopy has the ball.

hay **Hay** is **long, dried grass.** Linus is bringing Snoopy some hay to eat. Cows and horses like to eat hay. Snoopy likes almost every other kind of food.

---

he **He** is my friend.
That boy is my friend. **That man** is my friend.

---

head

Linus has fallen on his **head.** The head is the **top part of the body.** Your eyes, nose and mouth are parts of your head.

She is at the **head** of the line.
She is **first** in line.

---

health Roy has good **health.**
Roy is **not sick.**

When there is nothing wrong with your body, you are in good **health.** When there is something wrong with your body, your health is not good.

healthy Lucy is **healthy.**
Lucy is **well.**
Lucy is **not sick.**

---

hear I **hear** Schroeder playing the piano.
My ears receive the sounds that Schroeder makes on the piano.

heard I **heard** someone calling me.

heart

The picture on Snoopy's flag is in the shape of a **heart.** A heart is the **sign for love.**

The **heart** is really a **part of our body.** You can feel your heart beat.

---

heat **Heat** makes you feel warm. You can feel how hot the sun is by the way it **heats** you.

Mother will **heat** the water by boiling it on the stove.
Mother will **make the water hot** by boiling it on the stove.

---

heavy Something that is **heavy** is **not easy to lift.**

Something heavy means **thick and strong.**
I wear a heavy coat in winter.

205

heel The **heel** is the **back part of the foot.** I have two heels.

The **heel** of a shoe is the raised part of the shoe. It is on the bottom of the shoe. It is in the back of the shoe.

My socks also have **heels.**

---

hello We say **hello** when we meet someone we know.

---

help

Snoopy cannot reach the mailbox. He needs Charlie Brown **to help** him. He needs Charlie Brown **to make him able to reach** it. Charlie Brown **helps** Snoopy by letting him stand on his back.

I enjoy **helping** my father.
I enjoy **working with** my father so that he gets the job done sooner.

I **helped** him get the job done.

---

hen A **hen** is a grown mother **chicken.** Hens lay eggs.

---

her **Her** means **that girl** or **that woman.**
I would like to use Patty's skates. I will go and ask **her** if I may.

Her book means **that girl's** book.

here **Here** means **this place.**
Bring it **here,** please.
Bring it to **this place,** please.

---

hers The dress belongs to Violet.
The dress is **hers.** Hers means she owns it.

---

herself Sally hurt **herself** when she was jumping rope.
Sally hurt **her own body** when she was jumping rope.

She can do it **herself.**
She can do it **alone.**

---

hide

Snoopy has found a place to **hide.**
Snoopy has found a place where **no one can see him.**

He **hid** behind the tree so that Linus would not find him. He is almost **hidden** by the tree. He is almost **out of sight.**

---

high Lucy built a little hill for Charlie Brown to stand on, but it is too **high.**

The top of the hill is too **far off the ground.**

higher Snoopy is **higher** than Woodstock.
Snoopy is **farther up** than Woodstock.

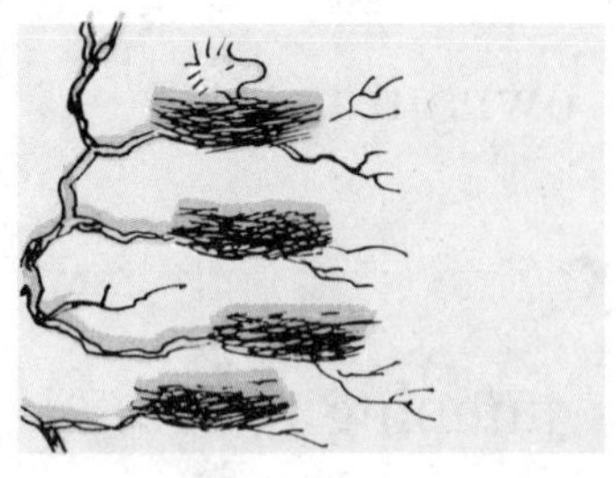

highest Woodstock lives in the **highest** nest in the tree.
There are nests in the tree below him, but none above him.

---

hill Peppermint Patty and Charlie Brown are standing on a **hill.** A hill is a piece of land that is higher than the land around it. It is not as high as a mountain.

---

him

Him means **that boy** or **that man.**
Snoopy is very fond of Charlie Brown. Snoopy pats him on the head.

---

himself Franklin wrapped **himself** up in the blanket.
Franklin wrapped **his own body** up in the blanket.

Roy sometimes plays by **himself.**
Roy sometimes plays **alone.**

his The dish belongs to Snoopy. The dish is **his.** His means **he owns it.**

---

hit

Pow! Did you see Lucy **hit** Linus? To hit someone is to **strike** him. Someday Lucy will learn that **hitting** people is not nice.

---

hive A **hive** is a little house that bees live in.

---

hockey **Hockey** is a game played on ice. You wear ice skates when you play hockey.

---

hog When a pig grows, he becomes a **hog.**

---

hold When Linus is tired or worried, he likes to **hold** his blanket. He likes to keep it in his hand. The blanket he is **holding** now is one of the blankets he **held** when he was a baby.

The lock **holds** the door shut.
The lock **keeps** the door shut.

hole There is a **hole** in the wall over Snoopy's bed. The hole is an **opening** you can see through.

I dug a **hole** in the ground.
I made an **empty place** in the ground by taking away the earth that was there.

---

holiday A **holiday** is a **special day** when people don't go to work or to school. Christmas is a holiday. So is Easter.

A **holiday** is also a **vacation.** We went to the country during our summer holiday.

hollow A balloon is **hollow.**
A balloon has **nothing in it but air.**

---

home Snoopy, come **home.**
Snoopy, come back to the **place where you live.**

---

honest Charlie Brown is **honest.**
Charlie Brown does not lie or steal. He tells the truth.

---

honey Bees make **honey.** Honey is sweet. I like to eat bread with honey on it.

---

honk The driver will **honk** at the boy on the bicycle.
The driver will **blow his horn** at the boy on the bicycle.

---

hood

Snoopy is wearing a **hood.** A hood is a **covering for the head.** We usually wear hoods when it rains or snows to protect our heads and necks.

---

hook Sally will hang her coat on a **hook.**
All the coats in Sally's closet are hanging on hooks. A hook is a **bent piece of wood or metal that holds things.** A fish hook catches and holds a fish.

hop

Look at Snoopy **hop.**
Look at Snoopy **jump on one foot.**

---

hope I **hope** to go with Mother. I **wish** to go with Mother.

---

horn A **horn** is a long, thin **instrument that a musician plays.** He blows into one end and sounds come out the other end.

The **horn** on our car makes a loud noise when anyone honks it.

Some animals have **horns** on their heads.

---

horse A **horse** is a large **animal** with long legs. **Horses** can run very fast. People can ride on horses. Some horses are very strong and can pull wagons or carriages. Linus made this drawing of a horse.

hose

A **hose** is a **long rubber pipe** that fastens to a faucet at one end. When we turn on the faucet, water comes out of the other end. Woodstock wants to water his garden with the garden hose. Firemen use a bigger hose to put water on a fire.

---

hospital People go to the **hospital** when they are sick. They go to the hospital to get well.

---

hot Be careful, Linus. The cup is **hot.** It feels **very warm** when you touch it. The sun is hot. Fire is hot. If you touch something hot, it will burn you.

---

hotel A **hotel** is a **place to live when you are away from home.** You can eat and sleep in a hotel. People pay money to live in a hotel.

---

hour An **hour** is a **measure of time.** There are sixty minutes in an hour. There are twenty-four hours in a day. You can tell what hour it is by the clock.

house Which **house** is yours, Charlie Brown?
Which is the **building in which you live,** Charlie Brown?

---

how The doctor says, "**How** are you? Do you feel good?" Then he says, "How old are you? How tall are you? How much do you weigh?"
Then he shows me **how** to stick out my tongue so that he can look at it. Then he shows me **the way** to stick out my tongue so that he can look at it.

---

hug Lucy is giving Charlie Brown a **hug.**
Lucy is throwing her arms around Charlie Brown and holding him tight. She is **hugging** him because she likes him very much.

hundred A dollar equals a **hundred** cents.
A dollar equals **100** cents.

---

hungry Charlie Brown and Linus are **hungry.**
Charlie Brown and Linus **want something to eat.** Their stomachs feel empty. They are very glad it's lunch time.

---

hunt I must **hunt** for my teddy bear.
I must **look for and try to find** my teddy bear.

If I keep **hunting** for my teddy bear, I will find him.

We **hunted** everywhere for the lost book.

---

hurrah Charlie Brown yelled, "**Hurrah,** we won!" Hurrah is a **happy shout.**

---

hurry "**Hurry,** Linus, you'll be late." To hurry is to **move as fast as you can.**

hurt

Lucy **hurt** her arm.
Lucy fell and **did harm** to her arm.

It **hurts** to fall on your arm.
It makes you **feel pain** when you fall on your arm.

---

husband A **husband** is a man a woman is married to. My father is my mother's husband. My father and mother are husband and wife.

---

hush I told Snoopy to **hush.**
I told Snoopy to **keep quiet.**

I i

I **I** am **me.** I am happy.

ice Snoopy is skating on **ice.** The water in the lake has turned to ice because it is very cold. Ice is water that is **frozen.**

ice cream **Ice cream** is Charlie Brown's favorite dessert. Ice cream is made of milk, eggs and sugar, mixed together and frozen. It tastes sweet and cold and creamy. Charlie Brown likes chocolate ice cream best and peach next best.

if "**If** you try, Snoopy, you can do it."
"**In case** you try, Snoopy, you can do it."

Snoopy doesn't know **if** he can learn.
Snoopy doesn't know **whether** he can learn.

ill

Linus is **ill.**
Linus is **sick.** He has a bad cold.

I'll **I'll** means **I will.** Violet wants to know if I will come to the party. Yes, I'll go.

I'm **I'm** means **I am.** Yes, I'm going to the party.

---

important Something that matters very much is **important.**
It's **important** that I know when you will return.
I have to know when you will return so that I can meet you.

---

in Snoopy is **in** bed with Charlie Brown.
Snoopy is **with** Charlie Brown under the covers.

I'll be there **in** a few minutes.
I'll be there **after** a few minutes.

Come **in.**
Come **inside.**

The letter was written **in** pencil.
The letter was written **by** pencil.

---

inch This line is one **inch** long ________ . One foot is equal to twelve **inches.** One yard is equal to thirty-six inches.

indeed I am glad **indeed.**
I am **really** glad.

Indian I like to pretend I'm an **Indian.** Indians were the **first Americans.** They lived in America before other people came.

---

ink We write with pen and **ink.** Ink is a **liquid that we use for writing.** Different color inks were used to make this book.

---

insect An **insect** is a **bug.** An ant is an insect. A fly is a flying insect. So is a mosquito.

---

inside

Linus is sitting **inside** a box.
He is **not outside** of it.
He likes being surrounded by the sides and top of the box.

---

instead Father took his book **instead** of his newspaper.
Father took his book **in place of** his newspaper.

---

instrument A **piano** is a **musical instrument.** It is a thing that makes music. Daddy needs a **tool** for hitting nails into a board. The instrument he chooses is a hammer.

interested Snoopy is **interested** in what he is reading.
The book holds his attention. He wants to know more about what he is reading.

---

into

Oops! Something fell **into** Snoopy's water dish.
It fell right **inside** Snoopy's water dish.

---

invite Charlie Brown has a list of all the people he wants to **invite** to his party To invite someone is to **ask** him **to come to visit** you. He **invites** Lucy first. He asks her to come to his party.
"I'll come," says Lucy, "if Schroeder is **invited.**"

---

iron **Iron** is a strong **metal.** There is an iron fence around the school yard.

Mother **irons** my clothes.
Mother **presses** my clothes **with an iron.**

island An **island** is a **piece of land with water all around it.**
We had to go in a boat to reach the island in the lake.

---

it

Woodstock is carrying a toy.
He is carrying **it** in his mouth.

it's The word **it's** with a little mark between the t and the s means **it is.**
It's time to go home.

its The word **its** without any mark means **belonging to it.**
See the rabbit. Its ears are very long.

---

itch A mosquito bite makes you **itch.** When something **itches,** you want to scratch it.

---

itself My paper doll will stand up by **itself.**
My paper doll will stand up **alone.**

I've **I've** means **I have.**
I've had a good time today.

J j

jacket Charlie Brown is wearing a **jacket.**
Charlie Brown is wearing a **short coat.**

jail A **jail** is a **building** with bars on the windows and doors. It is a place for people who have done bad things. The policeman takes the bad man to jail. He will be locked up so he can't get out.

jam Roy likes strawberry **jam** on his bread. His mother makes jam from all kinds of fruit.

January **January** is the **first month** of the year. It comes in the winter. It has thirty-one days. New Year's Day is the first day of January.

jar A **jar** is a **container** in which we keep food. Mother puts cooked fruit in a glass jar. She puts cookies in a cookie jar. She puts a cover on the jar and closes it tight to keep the food inside fresh and good.

---

jaw My **jaw** is the **lower part of my face.** My jaw moves when I chew food.

---

jelly Mother makes **jelly** from fruit juice and sugar. Most kids like jelly on their bread.

---

job

It is Charlie Brown's **job** to feed Snoopy every day.
Feeding Snoopy is the **work** that Charlie Brown must do every day.

---

join We **join** hands to make a circle.
We **put** our hands **together** to make a circle.

Linus wants to **join** Lucy's club.
Linus wants to **belong** to Lucy's club.

joke

Snoopy told Lucy a **joke.**
Snoopy told Lucy a **funny story.**
Lucy thought it was a bad joke. She didn't laugh.

The clown fell on his face. He did it as a **joke.**
He did it to be funny. He didn't hurt himself
The clown **joked** with us. He did funny things and made us laugh.

---

jolly Santa Claus is **jolly.**
Santa Claus is **full of fun.**

---

journey I went on a **journey** to see my aunt in another city.
I went on a **long trip** to see my aunt in another city.
When I take a journey, I go to a place away from home.

---

joy Lucy is full of **joy.**
Lucy is **very, very happy.**

---

juice I am squeezing the **juice** out of an orange. I will have a glass of orange juice. Sometimes I drink tomato juice.

juicy This orange has a lot of juice. It is very **juicy.**

July **July** is the **seventh month** of the year. It comes in the middle of the summer. It has thirty-one days. The Fourth of July is sometimes called Independence Day.

---

jump Snoopy has to **jump** from the roof of his house to the ground. He starts up, leaps into the air and lands on his feet. At first, he jumped too high and landed on his nose. But now Snoopy is very good at jumping.

June **June** is the **sixth month** of the year. It comes in the summer. It has thirty days.

---

just My shoes are **just** the right size.
My shoes fit me **exactly.**

Violet was given **just** praise for her drawing.
Violet was given the praise she **deserved** for her drawing.

K k

kangaroo The **kangaroo** is an **animal** that lives in Australia. It moves very fast by jumping on its strong back legs. Mother kangaroos carry their babies in a kind of pocket on their stomachs.

---

keep I will **keep** it safely in the box.
I will **take care of** it safely in the box.

Mother gave me a ring. I will **keep** it.
I will have it for a long time.

kept I have **kept** my teddy bear since I was a baby.

---

key A **key** is a small metal thing that goes into a lock and turns it. We turn the key to lock a door. We also turn the key to unlock a door. There are other kinds of keys that we press. When we press the keys of a piano, they make music.

kick

Why did Snoopy **kick** Schroeder?
Why did Snoopy **hit** Schroeder **with his foot?**

He **kicked** him when Schroeder wasn't looking.

Kicking people isn't nice. Sometimes it hurts.

---

kid A **kid** is a **baby goat.** It is also a short name for **a child.**

Roy says, "Come on, **kids.** Let's play tag."
Roy says, "Come on, **children.** Let's play tag."

---

kill I saw a cat **kill** a mouse.
I saw a cat **make** a mouse **die.**

---

kind My big brother is **kind** to us.
My big brother is **gentle and nice** to us.

What **kind** of pie do you like best?
What **sort** of pie do you like best?

---

kindergarten **Kindergarten** is **the grade before first grade.** In kindergarten all the children learn to play and work together. The kindergarten teacher shows them how.

king Some countries have a **king.** The king is the **leader** of the people in his country. Americans do not have a king. They have a President.

---

kiss

Lucy gave Snoopy a **kiss.** Lucy pressed her lips against Snoopy's to show him that she loved him.

She would have **kissed** him again, but Snoopy didn't want any more **kisses.**

He told Lucy to please stop **kissing** him.

---

kitchen Mother is working in the **kitchen.** Mother is working in the **room where our food is cooked.**

---

kite Charlie Brown is flying a **kite.** A kite is made of light wood covered with paper. It has a long string hanging from it. A kite is carried through the air by the wind.

kitten A **kitten** is a **young cat.** A mother cat may have several kittens.

---

kitty **Kitty** means **kitten.**

---

knee

The **knee** is the **joint in the middle of each leg.** We bend one knee at a time when we walk or go upstairs. We bend both knees when we jump. Linus is sitting on his **knees.**

---

knife A **knife** is used for cutting. It has a handle at one end and a sharp edge to cut with at the other.

knock **Knock** on the door, Charlie Brown. Then someone will hear you and open it for you.

I **knocked** against the table.
I **bumped** the table. I hit the table with my body.

knot I **tied** two pieces of rope together and made a **knot.**

My hair is **knotted.**
My hair is **tangled.**

---

know I **know** that I am six years old.
I **am sure** that I am six years old.

I **know** a poem.
I **have** a poem **in mind.**

I **knew** many of the children at the party.
I **had already met** many of the children at the party.

Schroeder **knows** that I am playing a trick on him.
Schroeder **understands** that I am playing a trick on him.

L l

lace My shoe **lace** is the **string** that ties my shoe.
I can **lace** my own shoes.

lad

Charlie Brown is a **lad.**
Charlie Brown is a **young boy.**

ladder Snoopy is standing on a **ladder.** He needs something tall to stand on so he can reach the top of the window. A ladder is a set of steps that you can move around and climb up on when you want to reach something that's very high.

lady My mother is a **lady.** My mother is a **woman.**

---

lake A **lake** is **water with land all around it.** In summer we swim in the lake.

---

lamb A **lamb** is a **baby sheep.** I saw a mother sheep and two little lambs.

---

lamp Lucy turned on the **lamp** so she could see better. It was getting dark and the lamp gives light. The light in Lucy's lamp comes from an electric bulb. Some lamps are lit by oil.

land

Snoopy is standing on **land.**
Snoopy is standing on the **shore.**

The United States of America is **my land.**
The United States of America is **the country I live in.**

The airplane **landed** in the field.
The airplane **came down** in the field.

---

lantern A **lantern** is a **light** that has glass or paper on every side to protect it from the wind. The farmer carries a lantern to light his way when he goes out at night.

---

lap

Doesn't Snoopy look comfortable with his head on Peppermint Patty's **lap?**
When you sit down, you make a lap from your waist to your knees.

Snoopy can **lap** his milk out of a dish. He **laps** it with his tongue. That is the way animals **drink.**

---

large Snoopy is sitting in a **large** boot.
Snoopy is sitting in a **very big** boot.

It is certainly **larger** than Snoopy's foot.

It is the **largest** boot I've ever seen.

last Snoopy is **last** in line.
Snoopy is **at the end** of the line. There is no one after him.

He arrived **last week.**
He arrived **the week before this one.**

How long will the movie **last?**
How long will the movie **go on?**

That is my **last** word.
That is my **final** word. I will not say any more.

---

late Linus was **late** for school.
Linus came **after the time** he was supposed to be in school. He was **tardy.**

Linus stayed up too **late** last night.
He stayed up after the time he usually goes to bed. So this morning he was late. He was **not on time.**

Linus was late, but Shermy was **later.**
Shermy came to school **after** Linus.

You go to the picnic now. I will come **later.**
I will come **after a while.**

---

laugh Charlie Brown must have said something funny to make Lucy **laugh.** She holds her sides and says, "Ha, ha, ha!" She is very happy. She cannot stop **laughing.** But Charlie Brown does not like to be **laughed** at. He doesn't think it is funny.

lawn Snoopy is cutting the **lawn.**
Snoopy is cutting the **grass in the yard.**

---

lay Roy will **lay** the book on the table.
Roy will **put** the book down on the table.

Hens **lay** eggs. Other birds lay eggs too.

laid I **laid** the book on the table.
I **placed** the book on the table.

---

lazy A **lazy** boy is a boy who does not want to work.

---

lead "Follow me, Charlie Brown," says Sally. "I will **lead** you to my secret hiding place." Sally will **guide** him there.

led She will go first and show him the way. She **led** him there once before, just as she is **leading** him there now.

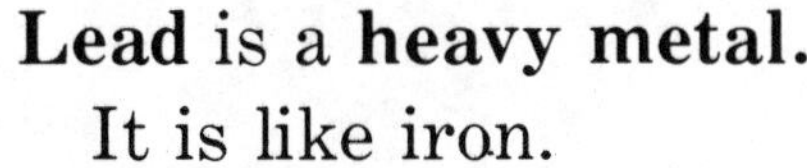

Lead is a **heavy metal.** It is like iron.

Another kind of **lead** is in a pencil. When you write with a pencil, you make letters with the lead. It is black.

---

leader Lucy was chosen **leader** of the team. A leader shows other people what to do. A leader tells other people what to do.

leaf "You made a **leaf** fall from the tree," says Lucy. "Now look what you did. Two **leaves** have fallen. If you don't stop shaking that tree there won't be any leaves left on it."
A leaf is **part of a tree or a plant.**

Sometimes the page of a book is called a **leaf.**

---

lean "**Lean** on me, Snoopy," says Charlie Brown. When Snoopy is tired, he just bends toward Charlie Brown and rests his head or whole body against him. Charlie Brown won't let him fall down.

---

leap What made Snoopy **leap** out of the mailbox?

leapt What made Snoopy **jump** out of the mailbox? He **leapt** out as fast as he could.

---

learn I will **learn** to write well.
I will **find out how** to write well.

leather **Leather** is made from the skin of an animal. My shoes are made of leather. Some coats and gloves are made of leather. Daddy's belt is made of leather. Snoopy's collar is made of leather.

---

leave Sally watches Charlie Brown **leave** the house.
Sally watches Charlie Brown **go away from** the house.

He **leaves** Sally home.
He does not take her with him.

Charlie Brown **left.**
Charlie Brown **went away.**

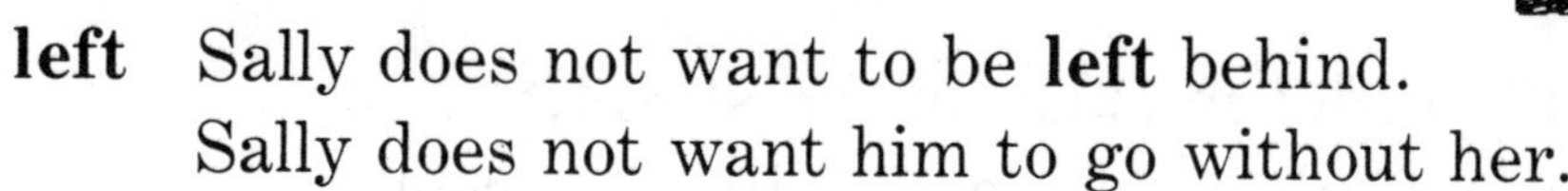

left Sally does not want to be **left** behind.
Sally does not want him to go without her.

---

left Charlie Brown raised his **left** arm. He kept his right arm at his side.

---

leg Lucy has one **leg** in the air. She is standing on her other leg. Will it hold her up? Snoopy has four legs to hold him up. Most animals have four legs. Chairs and tables have four legs too.

---

lemon A **lemon** is a yellow **fruit.** Lemons taste sour.

lemonade **Lemonade** is a very good **drink** made with lemon juice, sugar and water.

---

length The **length** of the ruler is twelve inches. The ruler is twelve inches long. It is twelve inches from one end of the ruler to the other end.

---

lesson My **lesson** today is on page ten of the book. My lesson is **what I must learn.**

---

let My mother will not **let** me play in the street. My mother will not **allow** me to play in the street.

---

let's **Let's** means **let us.** Let's play with our new kitty.

---

letter Charlie Brown is writing a **letter.** He is writing news about himself on a piece of paper. When he finishes his letter, he will put it in an envelope and mail it.

A is a **letter.** So is B and the other letters of the alphabet.

lettuce **Lettuce** is a leafy **vegetable.** We grow lettuce in our garden.

---

library

Charlie Brown and Sally have come to the **library** to get some books. A library is a place where many books are kept for people to read.

---

lick Linus will let Snoopy **lick** his hand.
Linus will let Snoopy **wet his hand with his tongue.** When Snoopy kisses someone, he licks him. When he eats, he licks his dish.

When someone says, "I can **lick** you," that means, "I can **win if I fight with you.**"

---

lid The **cover** on a jar, a pot or a box is called a **lid.**
We have **lids** on our eyes. They are called eyelids. When we close our **eyelids,** we cannot see.

lie I **lie** in my bed at night. My body is flat on the bed. When I lie in bed, I like to be covered with a warm blanket. Snoopy **lies** on the roof of his house.

lain Sally has **lain** down to take a nap, just as she
lay **lay** down yesterday.

lying Frieda is **lying** on her stomach to take a sunbath.

To tell a **lie** is to say **something that is not true.**
The boy is **lying.**
The boy is not telling the truth.

---

life A plant or an animal or a person has **life.** They all live and grow. A stone does not have life. An elephant has a long life. He lives a long time. A butterfly has a short life. It lives a short time. Something that looks very real is **lifelike.**

---

lift Charlie Brown can **lift** Snoopy.
Charlie Brown can **pick up** Snoopy.

---

light The sun makes **light.** An electric bulb makes light. When there is light we can see.

The feather is **light.**
The feather is **not heavy.**

Yellow is a **light** color.
Yellow is **not** a **dark** color.

---

lightning **Lightning** makes a very bright, quick light in the sky. Lightning and thunder often come when we have a rain storm.

like

Linus's snow-girl looks **like** Lucy.
Linus's snow-girl looks **almost the same** as Lucy.

Lucy does not **like** taking naps.
Lucy does not **enjoy** taking naps.

Lucy does not **like** Linus when he makes fun of her.
Lucy is **not happy with** Linus when he makes fun of her.

---

lily A **lily** is a pretty **flower.** Daddy gave Mother some lilies for Easter.

---

limb Linus broke off a **limb** of the tree.
Linus broke off a **branch** of the tree.

Sometimes we call an **arm** or **leg** a **limb.**

line Snoopy and the kids are standing in **line.**
Snoopy and the kids are standing **one behind the other in a row.**

Can you draw a straight **line?**
Can you make a **long, thin mark** with your pencil?

We have a telephone **line** going to our house. It is a **wire** that connects our phone to the other lines outside.

The **line** on my fishing rod is broken. I need a new **piece of string.**

---

lion A **lion** is a **wild animal.** The lion is called the king of the animals because he is so big and strong and fierce. There is a lion in the zoo. When the lion roars, it sounds like thunder.

---

lip Everybody has an upper **lip** and a lower **lip.** You make a circle with your lips when you whistle. Your **lips** are part of your mouth. When you open them your teeth can be seen.

---

liquid Water is a **liquid.** Milk is a liquid. So is gasoline. **Anything wet** that can be poured is a liquid.

listen

A good friend is someone who will **listen** to you. Snoopy listens to Sally. He **tries to hear** every word she says. He **pays attention** to what she is saying. It's nice to be **listened** to. "Thank you for **listening,** Snoopy," Sally says.

---

little

Sally is Charlie Brown's **little** sister.
Sally is Charlie Brown's **small** sister.

She is **littler** than he is.
She is **not as big** as he is.

She's the **littlest** person in the family.
She's **smaller than everyone else** in the family.

---

live

If I water my plant and keep it in the sun, it will **live** and grow. It will **not die.** It will **be alive.**

The birds live in a nest. We live in a house. We have **lived** in this house for ten years.

Beethoven is not still **living.** He died a long time ago.

load The truck has brought us a **load** of wood.
The truck has brought us a **pile** of wood.

I will **load** the wood on a wagon and pull it to the shed.
I will **pile** it on my wagon.

---

loaf Mother is baking a **loaf** of bread. When it is done, we will cut the loaf into slices. We will not keep the bread in one big piece. Sometimes Mother bakes two **loaves** at once.

---

lock When we **lock** our door it is closed tightly. The lock holds it shut. We can open it by putting a key in the lock and turning it. That unlocks the door.

Father keeps the doors to our house **locked** at night.

---

log "There's a spider on that **log,**" said Lucy to Linus, who was carrying a heavy load of **pieces of wood.** The wood came from a tree that was cut down and then cut in pieces. Each piece is called a log.

long Violet has **long** hair.
Violet's hair is **not short.**

The winter is **long.**
The winter **lasts for many months.**

Did Cinderella **long** to go to the ball?
Did Cinderella **want very much** to go to the ball?

I have waited for dinner a long time, but I will wait a little **longer.**

The red line is **longer** than the black one.

---

look Sally and Charlie Brown **look** around the door.
Sally and Charlie Brown **try to see** into the room.

They must **look** for something that is lost.
They must **try to find** something that is lost.

They **look** unhappy.
They **appear** unhappy.

They **look** at each other.
They **turn their eyes** toward each other.

What are they **looking** for?
Have they **looked** outside?

---

loose The wheel on my wagon is **loose.** It is **about to come off.** Father will fix it. He will fasten it tight.

There is a loose button on my coat. It is hanging by a thread. Mother will sew it on tight.

lose I must hold my money tight so I won't **lose** it. Mother pins my handkerchief on my dress so I won't lose it.

lost I **lost** my penny yesterday. I can't find it anywhere.

---

lot There are a **lot** of flowers in this field. It makes Woodstock happy to see so many flowers. The flowers are growing in a vacant **lot.** There used to be a building on this piece of land, but it was torn down.

---

loud Lucy has a **loud** voice. Something that **makes a lot of noise** is **loud.**
Schroeder's voice is not loud. It is quiet. His voice is not easily heard.
When we sing loudly, we are easily heard.

---

love Linus and Sally Brown **love** each other. They **like** each other **very, very much.** Linus shows Sally that he loves her by being very nice to her. He is **loving** to her. Everybody wants to be **loved.**

lovely Sally is a **lovely** girl.
Sally is a girl who is **easy to love.**

---

low My mother has a **low** voice.
My mother has a **soft** voice.

The airplane is flying **low.**
The airplane is flying **near the ground.**

The airplane is flying **lower** and lower. It is going to land.

Please **lower** the window shade.
Please **pull down** the window shade.

---

lump I have a **lump** on my head where I bumped it.
I have a **swelled place** on my head where I bumped it.

I fed the horse a **lump** of sugar.
I fed him a small **piece** of sugar.

---

lunch It's twelve o'clock noon and Charlie Brown is eating his **lunch.** Lunch is the **meal** we eat in the middle of the day.

---

lunch basket We carry our picnic lunch in a **lunch basket.**

M m

machine A **machine** is a thing with moving parts that does work faster and better than people can do it by hand. A sewing machine sews. A washing machine washes clothes. A vacuum cleaner is a machine that sweeps the floor. An automobile is a machine that takes us places quickly. What other machines can you think of?

---

mad Sometimes when we are **angry,** we say, "I'm **mad.**"

We do not go near a mad dog. It is very ill.

---

magic The good fairy in the story changed the pumpkin into a coach. That was **magic.** It happens only in stories.

The man in the show pulled a rabbit out of his hat. He said it was magic, but it was really a trick. Do you like to go to a show and see someone do magic tricks? Roy knows many tricks. He can fool his friends.

mail Linus has to **mail** a letter.
Lucy helps him **put the letter in the mailbox.**

We had a lot of **mail** this morning.
We had many **letters delivered to us.**

---

mailbox

The **box that holds mail** is called a **mailbox.**
Charlie Brown wonders if there is a letter for him in his mailbox.

---

mailman The man who brings the mail is the **mailman.**
He is also called a **postman.**

---

main The **main** show was in the big tent.
The **largest and best** show was in the big tent.

The **main** thing is to be on time.
The **most important** thing is to be on time.

make The children can **make** a snowman.
The children can **build** a snowman.

I will **make** a dress for my doll.
I will **sew** a dress for my doll.

I expect to **make** friends at my new school.
I expect to **get** many friends at my new school.

My father works to **make** money for our family.
My father works to **earn** money for our family.

If you run fast, it will **make** you tired.
If you run fast, you will **become** tired.

We **made** a bench yesterday.

Mother and I are **making** some cookies.

---

make believe To **make believe** is to pretend. I like to make believe I am a fireman.
Something that is **make-believe** is **not real.** A person in a story is a make-believe person.

---

male A **male** is a boy or a man. Father is a male. My brother is a male. Snoopy is a male dog.

---

mamma **Mamma** is a pet name for **Mother.** Baby loves her mamma.

---

man Daddy is a **man.** Charlie Brown is a boy. Charlie Brown will grow up to be a man like his daddy.

men Daddy and my uncle are **men.** Boys grow up to be men.

---

many

How can Snoopy eat so **many** dishes of food? He will get sick if he eats **such a large number** of things. That is a **lot** of food for a little dog.

---

map A **map** shows you where places are. It shows you where countries and oceans and towns and rivers are. The map of North America shows the United States and Canada. We may find our way with a road map when we drive in the car.

---

maple A **maple** is a kind of **tree.** Have you ever eaten maple sugar? It is made from a juice which comes out of the maple tree.

---

marble A **marble** is a very small ball made out of colored glass. There is a game you play with **marbles.**

Marble is a **hard kind of stone** that comes in big pieces. There is a marble floor in our school.

March **March** is the third **month** of the year. It comes at the end of winter. It has thirty-one days.

---

march The soldiers **march.**
The soldiers **walk in step** with each other.

---

mark Sally makes a **mark** on the sidewalk with chalk.
She makes a **spot** with chalk.

I got a good **mark** on my paper.
I got a good **grade** on my paper.

Mark an X on the paper.
Write an X on the paper.

---

market A **market** is a place where people buy things. We buy our fruit at the fruit market. We buy our meat at the meat market.

---

marry When a man and a woman **marry,** they become husband and wife.

Father and Mother were **married** in church.

marshmallow

A **marshmallow** is a soft, white kind of candy made with sugar, water and other things.

---

mask A **mask** is something you wear over your face so that no one will know who you are.
I wore a witch's mask on Halloween.

---

master A dog knows his **master.**
A dog knows his **owner.**

---

mat A **small rug** is sometimes called a **mat.** We wipe our feet on a door mat.

We put a **mat** under hot dishes when we put them on the table.

---

match Lucy and Patty and Charlie Brown have hats that **match.** All their hats **are alike.**

My ribbon matches my belt. They are both blue.

Father struck a **match** to light his pipe. Don't play with **matches.** They can burn you.

matter What is the **matter?**
What is the **trouble?**

It doesn't **matter** who goes first.
It doesn't **make any difference** who goes first.

May **May** is the fifth **month** of the year. It comes in the spring. It has thirty-one days. Memorial Day comes in May.

---

may Mother said, "You **may** go out and play."
Mother said, "You **are allowed** to go out and play."

We **may** have a picnic tomorrow if the weather is good.
We **will perhaps** have a picnic tomorrow if the weather is good.

---

maybe **Maybe** I can go, but I am not sure.
Perhaps I can go, but I am not sure.

---

me Mother said, "Who wants ice cream?" I said, **"I** do. Give it to **me."**

---

meadow A **meadow** is a **field.** Hay is grown in a meadow. Grass and flowers grow there too.

---

meal Breakfast is a **meal.** A meal is what we eat.

mean The boy was **mean** to his dog.
The boy was **not kind** to his dog.

What do you **mean?**
What do you **have in mind?**

My teacher asks, "What does this poem mean? Do you understand it? Do you know what it says?"

---

measure To **measure** means to find out the size or weight or amount of something.
Charlie Brown **measures** four feet. He is four feet tall.
One quart measures four cups. There are four cups in a quart.
How long is this stick? It measures six inches.

---

meat **Meat** is a **food.** It comes from animals. We have meat and vegetables for dinner.

---

medicine

Poor Snoopy. He is sick. The doctor gave him a bottle of **medicine** to make him well. If he takes his medicine, he will get to sleep and feel better tomorrow.

meet "Hello, I'm Franklin."
"Glad to **meet** you,"
said Linus.

met Linus and Franklin had not **met** before.
They had not **known each other** before.

Let's **meet** tomorrow.
Let's **get together** tomorrow.

See where those two buildings **meet.**
See where those two buildings **join.**

It was nice **meeting** you.
It was nice **getting to know** you.

---

melon A **melon** is a large **fruit** that grows on a vine. It is sweet and juicy inside. One kind of melon is watermelon.

---

melt Ice begins to **melt** when you hold it in your warm hand. Sugar will melt if you heat it in a pan. When something hard turns to a liquid, it **melts.**

When the sun began to shine, the snow **melted.** It turned into water.

---

mend Mother will **mend** my torn dress.
Mother will **sew up** my torn dress.

Father can **mend** my broken toy.
Father can **repair** my broken toy. He can fix it.

meow A cat says, **"Meow, meow."**

---

merry People are **merry** at Christmas time.
People are **laughing and happy** at Christmas time.

---

metal A **metal** is very hard. Most metals are heavy.
Iron, lead, silver and gold are metals.

---

middle My nose is in the **middle** of my face. It's in the **center** of it.

Our house is in the **middle** of the block. It is **between** each corner.

My **middle** finger is the longest finger on my hand.

---

mile It takes Charlie Brown and Sally twenty minutes to walk a **mile.** It is a mile to their school. There are 5,280 feet in one mile. It is many **miles** to the next town.

---

milk Linus is getting some **milk** to drink. Milk tastes good and is good for you. Our milk comes from cows. Have you ever seen anyone **milk** a cow?

milkman Our **milkman** brings us milk. He carries the bottles of milk in a wire basket.

---

mind Your **mind** tells you what to do. You think with your mind. You learn with your mind. You decide with your mind. You know with your mind.

Do you **mind** if we go out to play?
Do you **care** if we go out to play?

Mother says, "Please **mind** me, darling."
Mother says, "Please **obey** me, darling."

Sally will **mind** her dolls.
Sally will **take care of** her dolls.

---

mine The book is **mine.** I own the book. It is not yours, it is mine.

A **mine** is a **deep hole in the earth.** Coal comes out of a mine. Metal comes out of a mine.

---

minute A **minute** is a **measure of time.** There are sixty seconds in a minute. There are sixty minutes in an hour.

I will be there in a **minute.**
I will be there in a **very short time.**

The clock tells you that it is twenty **minutes** after eight.

mirror

Sally is looking at herself in the **mirror.** A mirror is a **looking glass.** Whatever is in front of the mirror shows in the glass.

Miss Our teacher is **Miss** Jones. She is not married, so we call her Miss.

---

miss

Charlie Brown will surely **miss** that ball. He will not hit it. Oops—he tried to hit it, but he **missed.**

Linus had been sick and almost had to **miss** the game. He almost **wasn't there.**

"We **missed** you, Linus," his friends said. "We wished you were here."

Now the children must hurry or they will **miss** the bus. They will **not catch** the bus before it leaves.

mistake When you do something wrong without meaning to, it is a **mistake.** I put your cap on by mistake. I thought it was mine.

I made a mistake in writing my name. I did not write every letter in my name.

---

mitten Lucy is wearing **mittens** on her hands to keep them warm. A **mitten** has two pockets—one for the thumb and one for the rest of the fingers. Lucy thinks mittens are warmer than gloves.

---

mix Sometimes I **mix** flour and water to make paste. Sometimes I **stir together** flour and water to make paste.

The children **mix up** their mother when they ask her to do so many things at once. She doesn't know what she is doing.

---

moment I will be there in a **moment.** I will be there in a **minute.** I will be there in a **very short time.**

Monday **Monday** is the second **day** of the week.

---

money A half-dollar is **money.** A quarter is money. A dime is money. A dollar bill is paper money. You pay for things with money.

My mother gives me a penny to spend on candy. I earn money when I work.

---

monkey A **monkey** is a funny **animal.** Have you seen monkeys at the zoo? I like to watch them play together. They hang by their tails and leap through the air.

Sometimes Daddy says, "Don't **monkey** with that." Sometimes Daddy says, "Don't **touch or play** with that."

---

month A **month** is a **part of the year.** There are twelve months in a year. They are January, February, March, April, May, June, July, August, September, October, November and December.

---

moo The cow says, **"Moo, moo."**

---

moon

There is a full **moon** shining tonight. Snoopy can see a whole **circle of light in the sky.** Sometimes we see only part of the moon. Then the night is not so bright.

---

moonlight When the moon shines at night, we have **moonlight.** Moonlight is not as bright as sunshine.

more I was tired but my sister was **more** tired than I was.

Sally said, "I want more milk." Charlie Brown said, "I want more cake." Snoopy begged for more meat. Mother gave them each another thing to eat or drink.

---

morning The **first part of the day** is **morning.** The sun is coming up. It is morning. I wake up in the morning and eat my breakfast. We go to school in the morning. I help my mother dust the house every morning.

---

mosquito A **mosquito** is a **flying insect.** It can bite people. Mosquito bites itch.

---

most These dolls are beautiful, but this doll is the **most** beautiful of all. It is more beautiful than the others.

When you divide the cake, give Mother the **most.**
When you divide the cake, give Mother the **largest part.**

Lucy had **most** of the apples.
Lucy had **nearly all** of the apples.

---

mother I love my **mother.** My mother takes care of me. She is married to my father. My mother and father are husband and wife. They are my parents.

mountain

A **mountain** is a **very big hill.** Some mountains have snow on top. No one can jump over a mountain. Snoopy is only dreaming about leaping from mountain to mountain.

---

mouse A **mouse** is a little **animal** with big ears and a long tail.

mice I saw two **mice** run into a hole.

---

mouth Sally opens her **mouth** wide when she cries. Big sounds come out of her mouth. We talk with our mouths and we eat with our mouths. A bird's mouth is called his bill.

move Will you **move** the table for me?
Will you **put** the table **in a different place** for me?

We will **move** soon.
We will **go to a different place** soon.

I **moved** the table for her.

The men are **moving** our furniture.

---

movie We went to see a **movie.** We went to see a **show** about Mickey Mouse. We sat in a dark theater and looked at **moving pictures.** It's fun to go to the **movies.**

Mr. My father is **Mister** Brown. This is a short way to write it: **Mr.** Brown.

Mrs. My mother writes her name this way: **Mrs.** R. J. Brown. She writes Mrs. because she is a married woman.

---

much How **much** money do you have? What **amount** of money do you have?
How much is left of the cake?
Do you have much time to help me? Do you have **a lot** of time to help me?
I don't like this book very much.

---

mud Dirt and water together make **mud.** My shoes got dirty in the mud.

muddy Schroeder's rubbers are **muddy.** He has been walking in the mud.

music Schroeder loves **music.** He makes music on his piano all day. Lucy doesn't like the sounds that Schroeder makes. She would rather he play **songs** that she could sing.

---

must You **must** drink your orange juice.
You **have to** drink your orange juice.

---

my See **my** pencil. It belongs to me. It is not your pencil.

---

myself I saw the rabbit **myself.** I hurt myself when I fell down.

I don't like to walk to school by **myself.**
I don't like to walk to school **alone.**

I tied my shoe myself.
Nobody did it for me.

N n

nail Daddy is holding a **nail** in his hand. He is going to hit it into the wood with a hammer. The nail keeps the two pieces of wood together. It joins the pieces of wood.

---

name What is your **name?**
What are you **called?**

My name is Sally Brown. What name did your father and mother give you? What is your last name?

What is the name of that tree? It is called an oak tree. Oak is its name.

What did you **name** your puppy? We **named** the puppy Chips.

nap Charlie Brown is taking a **nap.** He is taking a **short sleep.** What a funny place to nap. Have you ever seen anyone napping on a bench where the bus stops?

---

napkin Frieda wipes her mouth with a **napkin.** A **napkin** is a piece of cloth or paper we use when we eat. We use it to clean our lips or our fingers.

---

narrow The path we walked on was **narrow.**
The path we walked on was **not wide.** The street is wide, but the sidewalk is narrow.

naughty He was a **naughty** boy.
He was a **bad** boy.

---

navy A **navy** is all the fighting ships of a country and the men that run them. My uncle is in the navy. The men in the navy are called sailors. Our navy fights on the sea when we are at war.

---

near The horse is **near** the fence, but far away from the tree.
The horse is **close to** the fence, but far away from the tree.

---

nearly Sally is **nearly** as tall as her brother.
Sally is **almost** as tall as her brother.

It is nearly time to go to bed.

---

neat Patty keeps her room **neat.**
Patty keeps her room **clean and in order.**

Do you try to keep your room and your clothes neat?

---

neck Snoopy wears a collar around his **neck.** Your head is above your neck. Your shoulders are below your neck.

---

necktie Daddy wears a **necktie** around his neck. A necktie looks like a wide, heavy ribbon that ties in a knot at the neck and hangs down in front.

need I **need** a knife to cut the string.
I **should have** a knife to cut the string.

I **need** your help.
I **must have** your help.

I was cold. I **needed** my coat to keep me warm.

---

needle We sew with a **needle** and thread. A needle has a tiny hole in it. The thread goes through the hole. A needle looks like a pin without a head.

---

neighbor Any person who lives near me is my **neighbor.**

---

neither Both Linus and Schroeder ran in the race, but **neither** of them won.
Both Linus and Schroeder ran in the race, but **not either one** of them won.

The arrow went neither to the right nor the left. It went straight to the center of the tree trunk.

---

nest While Snoopy slept, some birds built a **nest** on his stomach. Birds live in nests. Most birds build their own nests from bits of branches, mud and leaves. Mother birds lay eggs in their nests.

net Snoopy is going fishing with a rod and a **net.**

The net looks like a piece of cloth with holes in it.
The fish goes into the net and
the water goes out through the holes.
Some people catch butterflies with a net.

There is a big **net** across the tennis court. It makes a fence between the two sides of the court.

---

never I can **never** jump that high.
I can **not ever** jump that high.

---

new Frieda has a **new** coat. Lucy has an old coat.

I will go to a **new** school when we move.
I will go to a **different** school when we move.

---

news Father reads the **news** in the paper.
Father reads the **story of what has happened** in the paper.

We all watched the **news** on television.

newspaper

Charlie Brown is reading a **newspaper.** He is reading the news about yesterday's baseball game. There is a picture of the players in the newspaper. You read about things that happened yesterday in the newspaper.

New Year's Day **New Year's Day** is the first day of January. It is the first day of the new year.

---

next Linus and Snoopy are in bed **next** to Charlie Brown. They are **beside** him.

Next time they will sleep at Linus's house.
The time after this one they will sleep at Linus's house.

---

nice Our house is **nice.** It is **pretty and pleasant** to live in. My clothes are **nice.** They are clean and fit me well. Violet is **nice.** She is **kind and fun to be with.**

---

nickel A **nickel** is money. A nickel will buy five cents' worth.

---

night At **night** it is dark. During the day it is light. At night I go to bed. I sleep most of the night.

nightgown I wear a **nightgown** to bed.
I wear a **night dress** to bed.

---

nine **Nine** is the number that comes after eight. Let's count to **9:**
1 2 3 4 5 6 7 8 **9.**

---

no Linus had **no** gloves.
Linus had **not any** gloves.

I asked Father if I could go swimming. He said, "**No,** it's too cold today."

---

nobody I heard something in the room, but **nobody** was there.
I heard something in the room, but **no person** was there.

---

nod I **nod** when someone asks me a question. I move my head down and up. I mean "Yes."

Sometimes when Grandfather is sleepy, his head will **nod.**

---

noise

Snoopy hit the pan with his bone and made a loud **noise.**
He made a loud **sound.**

I hear **noises** in the street. I hear the **sounds** of automobile horns honking and dogs barking.

none We looked for flowers. There were **none.** There were **not any.**

---

noon We go to lunch at **noon.** We go to lunch at **twelve o'clock in the middle of the day.**

---

nor Charlie Brown had neither his coat **nor** his cap on. He did not wear a cap **or** a coat.

---

north Point your right hand to where the sun comes up. Point your left hand to where the sun goes down. Look straight ahead. You will be looking toward the **north.** On a map, north is at the top.

---

nose Charlie Brown hit Lucy on the **nose.**
He hit her on the **thing that sticks out in the middle of her face.**

We breathe through the two holes in our **noses.**
We smell things through our noses.

---

not Mother and I will go to the movies. Baby will **not** go to the movies. We had to say **"No"** to her.

note I wrote a **note** of thanks.
I wrote a **short letter** of thanks.

Mother made a **note** of what she needs to buy.
Mother **wrote down** what she needs to buy.

---

nothing Franklin opened the box. There was **nothing** in it.
There was **not a thing** in it.

---

notice

"**Notice** that worm, Linus," said Lucy.
"**Look at** it."

Linus did not **notice** anything.
Linus did not **see** the worm.

November **November** is the eleventh **month** of the year. It comes in the autumn. It has thirty days. Thanksgiving comes in November.

---

now The telephone is ringing **now.**
The telephone is ringing **at this time.**

number

Here are two boys. Two is the **number** of boys. A number tells **how many.**

They have a large number of books.
They have a hundred books.

This is the number of our house: 421. The number is part of our address. We live at 421 Main Street.

Here are numbers from one to ten:
1 2 3 4 5 6 7 8 9 10.

---

nurse A **nurse** takes care of sick people. A nurse took care of me when I was in the hospital.

---

nut **Nuts** have hard shells and grow on trees or plants. The inside of a **nut** is good to eat. I like to eat peanuts. I break open the shell and eat the **seed** inside.

oak An **oak** is a kind of **tree.**

oatmeal I eat **oatmeal** for breakfast. It is made from oats. My mother cooks it for us.

oats The **oats** are growing in the field. The grains from oats are used for food. Oats are a very good food for horses.

obey I **obey** my father. I **do what he says** I must do. I taught my dog to obey me. He does what I tell him to do.

ocean The **ocean** is the largest **body of water** there is. Ships travel on the ocean.
The Atlantic Ocean touches the east shore of America.
The Pacific Ocean touches the west shore of America.

o'clock It is ten **o'clock.**
It is ten **by the clock.**

October **October** is the **tenth** month of the year. It comes in the autumn. October has thirty-one days. Halloween is the last day in October.

---

of The skirt **of** my blue dress is too short.
The skirt **that belongs to** my blue dress is too short.

The stories **of** A. A. Milne are interesting to children.
The stories **by** A. A. Milne are interesting to children.

The big hill is a mile north **of** town.
The big hill is a mile north **from** town.

The king's crown **of** gold is heavy.
The king's crown **made from** gold is heavy.

He was a man **of** good sense.
He was a man **having** good sense.

Tell me the story **of** Little Red Riding Hood.
Tell me the story **about** Little Red Riding Hood.

It is ten minutes **of** nine.
It is ten minutes **before** nine.

off

Sally got **off** the bus. She was on the bus and she got **down from** it.

The light was on and I turned it **off.** Now there is no light.

I took **off** my hat.
I took it **from** my head.

---

office An **office** is a **place where people work.** The principal at our school has an office. Daddy writes at a desk in his office. Sometimes we mail our letters at the post office.

---

often **Often** means **many times.**
I often go downtown. Sometimes I go once a week.
I wash my hands often. Sometimes I wash them ten times a day.

---

oh Sally said, **"Oh, oh!"** She was surprised to see the beautiful Christmas tree.

---

oil At the gas station they put **oil** in the car. Oil is a slippery liquid that helps make the car and other machines run.
Oil is also used for cooking.

old Grandmother is **old.** She is **not young.**

I am six years **old.**
I am six years **of age.** In two years I will be as old as my brother is now. I am old enough to go to school.

My shoes are too old to wear. I got some new ones.

My brother is eight years old. He is **older** than I am.
My sister is the **oldest** child in our family. She is twelve years old.

---

on Where is the doll? It is **on** a chair. The kitty is on her pillow.
When are you going to the circus? Are you going on Tuesday?

What is your book **about?** It looks like a book **on** birds.

The lights were off, but Mother turned them on.
I will go on reading the story until I finish it.

---

once I have seen a wild bear only **once.**
I have seen a wild bear only **one time.**

All the children spoke **at once.**
All the children spoke **at the same time.**

Once upon a time there was a king who had three daughters.
A long time ago there was a king who had three daughters.

one A man has **one** nose, one mouth and **a** head.

This is the number one: 1.
1 2 3 4 5 6 7 8 9 10 11 12

One should be careful when crossing the street.
A person should be careful when crossing the street.

---

one hundred There are **one hundred** cents in a dollar.
There are **100** cents in a dollar.

---

onion An **onion** is a **vegetable.** When you peel onions, tears come from your eyes. There are different kinds of onions. Some are yellow, some are green, some are white and some are red. I can smell onions cooking.

---

only This is the **only** road up the mountain.
There is **no other** road up the mountain.

I have **only** one penny.
I have **just** one penny and no more.

I am an **only** child.
I have no brothers or sisters.

---

open The mailbox is **open.**
It is **not closed.**

Charlie Brown **opened** it.
He **took the cover off** the front of the mailbox.

There is a letter for him. He **opens** it.
He takes it out of the envelope and **unfolds** it.

---

or Do you want to play outdoors **or** indoors? Do you want milk or water to drink? You can choose one of the two.

---

orange An **orange** is a **fruit** We drink orange juice for breakfast. My mother squeezes the **oranges** to make orange juice.

The color orange was named for the fruit.

---

order We put the blocks away in **order** of size.
We put the biggest blocks at one end and the smallest blocks at the other end.

My room is **in order.**
Everything is **in the right place.**

The captain gave the sailors an **order.**
He told them **what they had to do.**

Mother **orders** things from the butcher.
She tells the butcher what she wants him to send.

---

other I will wear the **other** coat today.
I will wear a **different** coat today.

Have you any **other** marbles?
Have you any **more** marbles?

I stayed home and all the **other** children went to the movies.
I stayed home and **all the rest** of the children went to the movies.

Charlie Brown ran up every **other** step.
Charlie Brown ran up every **second** step.

---

ouch I hurt my finger. I said, **"Ouch!"**

---

ought We **ought** to help Mother.
We **should help** Mother. It's the right thing to do.

---

our Snoopy is **our** dog. He belongs to us.

---

ours Snoopy is **ours.** Rover is yours.

---

ourselves We have a playhouse. We fixed it up **ourselves.**
We did it **without help** from anybody else.

My brother and I were standing by **ourselves** away from the others.
My brother and I were standing alone away from the others.

out

Linus pulled something **out** of the bag to show Lucy.
He took it **from inside** the bag.

Snoopy is coming **out** of his house.

Mother was not home. I told the man at the door, "My mother is **out.**"
I went **out** with my brother, and we played baseball with the boys.
When the lights are **out,** the room is dark. We turn the lights out every night when we go to bed.

---

outdoors

Snoopy is **outdoors.**
He is **not in the house.**

Snoopy likes to sit **outdoors** on the grass at night. He likes to be **in the fresh air.**

He stays outdoors until it gets cold. Then he goes indoors.

---

outside

Charlie Brown is **outside** the door.

He is on the side of the door that is outdoors. His books are inside.
The outside of his house is white. The inside is mostly yellow.
Sometimes people say outside when they mean outdoors.

oven My mother bakes bread in the **oven.** The oven is **part of the stove.**

---

over

Snoopy jumped **over** a rose bush to get away from Lucy.
He jumped right **across** it.

I hold an umbrella **over** my head when it rains.
I hold it **above** my head.

The party is **over,** and we must go home.
The party is **at an end,** and we must go home.

Be careful of the milk bottle or you will tip it **over.**

There is snow all **over** the ground.

My sister had to write the letter **over** and over.
My sister had to write the letter **again** and again.

Daddy has **over** five dollars.
Daddy has **more than** five dollars.

overalls I wear **overalls** when I play.
I wear long pants with a part that covers my stomach and goes over my shoulders.

Daddy wears **overalls** when he cleans the basement. They cover his other clothes and keep them clean.

---

owl An **owl** is a **bird** with big eyes. "Who-o-o" says the owl. Owls fly at night.

own This book is my **own.** It belongs to me. The other is a library book. It does not belong to me. It is not my own.

I **own** twelve books.
I **have** twelve books that belong to me.

John **owned** five rabbits.

---

ox An **ox** is an **animal** that looks something like a cow. An ox is sometimes used to pull a small wagon.

oxen When one ox and another ox pull together, we say, "That is a team of **oxen.**"

P p

pack The man is carrying a **pack** on his back.
The man is carrying a **bundle** on his back. He is going to camp in the woods.

The men **pack** the tomatoes in boxes.
The men **put** the tomatoes in boxes.

I pack my suitcase when I go away.

package Linus wonders what is in the **package.**
What is in the **box that is all wrapped up?** Could it be a gift from Lucy? Linus likes to get **packages.**

paddle

It's hard work **to paddle** a canoe.
It's not easy **to push** the canoe **through the water.**

When you hold the handle of **the paddle** and push the flat, wide part against the water, the boat moves forward.
Charlie Brown would rather have Snoopy's job.

page I am writing my name on the first **page** of my book. I will be careful when I turn each page of my book.

There are many **pages** in this book. Most of the pages have pictures. Do you like to turn the pages and look at the pictures? Each piece of paper in the book is a page.

---

pail

Sally Brown is filling her **pail** with sand. A pail is used to hold water or sand.

We play with **pails,** and my father uses a pail when he helps wash the floor.

---

pain Linus has a **pain** in each foot.
His feet **hurt.**
Did you ever have a toothache?
A toothache is a pain in a tooth.

---

paint There are many different colors of **paint.** I have a can of red paint. Paint is used to color things.

I will **paint** my wagon red.
I will **color** my wagon red with paint.

Lucy **painted** a picture. She used many colors of paint.
My mother is **painting** the baby's high chair.

---

pair A **pair** is **two of a kind.** You wear a pair of shoes. You wear a pair of gloves. We have a pair of kittens. They are both little and black.

pajamas

Sally is going to bed.
She wears **pajamas** when she sleeps.
Pajamas are a kind of clothes we wear when we go to sleep.

---

palace The king lived in a **palace.**
The king lived in a **large and beautiful house.**

---

pan My mother bakes a cake in a cake **pan.** She fries eggs in a frying pan. A pan is a flat pot used for cooking.

---

pancake A **pancake** is flat and round. It is made of milk, eggs and flour. Linus likes to eat **pancakes** with butter on them.

---

pansy A **pansy** is a small **flower** with big petals. **Pansies** grow in many beautiful colors.

---

pant Snoopy will **pant** if he is too hot.
Snoopy will **breathe fast** if he is too hot.

pants Linus is putting on his **pants.** Pants are also called **trousers.**

papa **Papa** is a pet name for **father.**

paper

This is a letter for Charlie Brown. It is written on **paper.** This book is made of paper. We wrap packages with wrapping paper. There is wallpaper on the walls of our rooms.

parachute A man uses a **parachute** when he wants to jump out of an airplane. The parachute is fastened to his body. It opens out when he jumps. The parachute makes him float down to the ground slowly.

---

parade Have you ever seen a circus **parade?** Animals and people in bright costumes march to music. Sometimes soldiers have a parade. They march in straight lines past the captain.

---

pardon "**Pardon** me, I didn't mean to bump you."
"**Excuse** me, I didn't mean to bump you."

---

park The **park** has beautiful trees and green lawns. We often take a walk in the park. Linus likes to feed the birds in the park.

Father will **park** the car here.
Father will **put** the car here.

---

part Charlie Brown cut a **part** of the pie and put it on his plate.
He put a **piece** of the pie on his plate.

Our bodies have many **parts.** The head is a part of the body. The arm is another part.

We will **part** at the corner.
I will go one way and you will go the other way.

---

party On my birthday I had a **party.** When friends get together to eat and play, it is a party.
We played games and had ice cream and cake to eat.

pass The car will **pass** the bus.
The car will **go on by** the bus.

Please **pass** me the meat.
Please **hand** me the meat.

The clouds will soon **pass,** and the sun will shine again.
The clouds will soon **move on,** and the sun will shine again.

I work hard in school so that I will **pass.**
I work hard in school so that I will **go on to the next grade.**

The parade **passed** our house.
The parade **went by** our house.

---

past It is **past** one o'clock. It is **after** one o'clock.

Winter is **past.** It is now spring.
Winter has **gone by.** It is now spring.

---

paste **Paste** is used to stick paper together. You can make one kind of paste by mixing flour and water.

I like to **paste** pictures in a book.
I like to **stick** pictures in a book with paste.

---

pasture The horses are eating grass in the **pasture.**
They are in a **field** with a fence around it.

---

pat Charlie Brown is watching Linus **pat** the bird on the head.
Linus **taps** the bird's head **very gently** with his open hand. He **pats** the bird's head to show that he likes him.

patch Sally Brown has a **patch** over her eye.
She has a small **piece of cloth** covering her eye.

Mother sewed **patches** on the knees of my pants.
The patches cover the holes that I tore in them.

---

path "Let's take this **path,**" said Charlie Brown to Linus.
They walk along **a dirt walk** with nothing growing on it.

Horses run on a bridle **path.** It is a **dirt road** made by the feet of many horses.

---

paw Snoopy is holding up his front **paw.**
A paw is the **foot of an animal**, with claws. Most animals have four paws.

---

pay

Charlie Brown will **pay** for his ticket to the movies.
Charlie Brown will **give money** for his ticket to the movies.

Every week Daddy gets his **pay.**
Every week Daddy gets his **money for working.**

paid My mother **paid** me for cutting the grass.

---

peach A **peach** is a **fruit.** It has a soft yellow skin and is juicy inside. May we have **peaches** for supper?

peanut A **peanut** is a **plant.** The seeds grow in shells under the ground. We eat the seeds.

---

peanut butter **Peanut butter** tastes like peanuts, but it is smooth and as easy to spread as butter. I like to eat peanut butter sandwiches.

---

pear A **pear** is a **fruit.** It grows on a pear tree. Would you rather have a peach or a pear?

---

peas Green **peas** are one of the **vegetables** I like best. They are really the seeds of the pea plant.

---

peck Watch the chicken **peck** at its food.
Watch the chicken **strike at and pick up** its food.

The woodpecker can **peck** a hole in the bark of a tree.
He can **strike** a hole in the tree.

---

peel Mother will **peel** the apple for me.
Mother will **take off the skin** of the apple for me.

---

peep Baby will **peep** through her fingers if I say, "Peek-a-boo."
Baby will **look** through her fingers if I say, "Peek-a-boo."

Baby birds say, **"Peep, peep."**

---

pen Charlie Brown is writing with his **pen.**
A pen makes marks on paper with ink.

The farmer keeps his pigs in a **pen.**
The farmer keeps his pigs in a **small fenced yard.**

pencil

Charlie Brown is drawing with a **pencil.** A pencil makes marks on paper with lead.

---

penny A **penny** is a **cent.** What can you buy with a penny?

What can you buy with five **pennies?** What can you buy with five cents? Five pennies are worth a nickel.

---

people Many **people** were at the movies. Many **persons** were at the movies.

---

perfect Franklin's letter was **perfect.** His letter had **no mistakes.** He wrote all the words in the right way.

Will you pick me a **perfect** peach? Will you pick me a peach that has **nothing wrong** with it?

---

perhaps I think **perhaps** I shall get a letter. I think it **may be** that I shall get a letter.

---

person I am a **person.** You are a person. Everyone is a person.

---

pet A **pet** is an **animal** that you take care of and play with. Snoopy is Charlie Brown's pet.

I have three pets. I have a cat and a pony and a bird.

petal A **petal** is the brightly colored **leaf** of a flower.

---

pet name A **pet name** is a special name that you give to someone you love. It is not the person's real name. Grandma is a pet name for Grandmother.

---

piano A **piano** is a **musical instrument.** Schroeder loves to play the piano. He strikes the keys and lovely tunes come out.

Here comes Lucy to hear Schroeder make music on his piano.

---

pick I will **pick** the apples.
I will **pull** the apples **off** the tree with my fingers.

Which boys do you **pick** to play on your team?
Which boys do you **choose** to play on your team?

We **picked** a bunch of flowers for Mother.

picnic Snoopy and Frieda are having a **picnic.** They are having a **meal outdoors.** They sit on the grass to eat their lunch and drink their milk. Picnics are fun.

---

picture Everyone in the class drew a **picture,** and the teacher hung all the pictures on the wall. Linus drew a picture of a house and a tree with colored crayons. Lucy painted a picture of a little girl.

---

pie Mother baked an apple **pie.** She put some thin dough in a round pan and put apples and sugar on top. Then she covered it with more dough and put the pie in the oven. When the pie was brown, she took it out and cut a piece for me to eat.

---

piece

Charlie Brown is angry at Lucy for eating the last **piece** of cake. There was a whole cake yesterday but everybody took **pieces** of it until there was only one **part** left. "You could have left a little bit," shouts Charlie Brown.

---

pig A **pig** is a **young hog.** Have you ever seen a little pig with its mother? There are many **pigs** on our farm.

pile This is a **pile** of wood.

We **pile** our wood in the garage.
We put one log on top of another log, until we have many logs in a bunch.

pillow

Linus sleeps with his head on a **pillow.** His pillow is filled with feathers and is very soft. He's trying to stay awake, but his head falls down on the pillow and soon he is asleep.

pilot A **pilot** of an airplane is the man who flies it.

Snoopy likes to make believe he is a pilot.

A ship's pilot keeps the ship on her course.

pin A **pin** is a very small, thin, metal stick with a sharp point. It is used to fasten things together. Mother uses pins when she sews.
I have a pretty pin made of gold.

I will **pin** a flower on you.
I will **fasten** a flower on you with a pin.

pine Behind Snoopy and the tent are **pine** trees. A pine tree is green all year round. Many pine trees are called a forest of **pines**

---

pink Lucy's dress is **pink**. Pink is a **color** made by mixing red and white.

---

pint There are two cups in a **pint.** I was so thirsty that I drank a pint of milk.

---

pipe City water comes out of a **pipe.** Gas goes through a pipe. Pipes are also used to carry oil all over the United States of America.

Father smokes a **pipe.**

pitcher We pour from a **pitcher.** A pitcher has a handle. We use a big pitcher for water. We use a little pitcher for cream. Pitchers hold liquid.

A baseball **pitcher** throws the ball to the man who is at bat. My father took me to a baseball game. The pitcher threw a fast ball.

---

place My **place** at the table is where I sit at the table.

My toys are in the toy box. That is **the place** for them. That is **where they should be.**

I scratch my leg in two **places.**
I scratched my leg in two **spots.**

I have lost my **place** in the book. I can't find where I stopped reading.

New York is a **place** I would like to see.
New York is a **city** I would like to see.

I will **place** my doll in her chair.
I will **put** my doll in her chair.

I **placed** the dishes on the table.

---

plain The man spoke in **plain** words.
The man spoke in **easy** words.

My new dress is too **plain.** It does not have enough trimming to make it look pretty.

A **plain** is **smooth and flat country.** Cowboys ride on the plains.

plan Father gave me a **plan** for a boat.
He gave me a **drawing that shows how** the boat is to be built.

We **plan** to go. We **expect** to go.

We will **plan** our trip before we go.
We will **think out** our trip before we go.

---

plane An airplane is sometimes called a **plane.** The **planes** fly over our house on their wav to the airport.

---

plant A rose bush is a **plant.** Bushes, trees, grass, vegetables and flowers are all called **plants.**

The farmer will **plant the seeds.**
The farmer will **put the seeds in the ground.**

Factories are sometimes called **plants.**

We **planted** the seeds this morning. The seeds that we planted will grow into beautiful flowers.

---

plate Mother put my lunch on a **plate.**
Mother put my lunch on a **dish.**

---

play Schroeder likes to **play** the piano.
He likes to **make music** on the piano.

Lucy would like him to **play** with her instead.
Lucy would like him to **join** her **in some fun.**

I acted in a **play.**
I acted in a **show.**

I **played** a clown.
I **pretended to be** a clown.

The cat is **playing** with a ball.
The cat is **having fun** with a ball.

player A **player** is **anyone who plays a game.** We need another player for our baseball team.

Players also act in shows.

---

playground We play on the **playground** at school or in the park. The playground of our school has swings and seesaws in it.

---

playhouse Sally has a **playhouse.** A playhouse is like a real house, but much smaller.

---

playmate Your **playmate** is the boy or the girl you play with.

---

pleasant We spent a **pleasant** evening at the park. We spent an evening **that pleased** us at the park.

---

please When we ask for something, it's nice to say, **"Please."** "Please, may I have some cake?"

It will **please** my mother if I am polite to her friend. It will **make** my mother **feel good** if I am polite to her friend.

I am **pleased** to meet you.
I am **glad** to meet you.

That is a **pleasing** song. I like the sound of it.

---

plenty There is **plenty** of milk.
There is **all** the milk **that is needed.**

plow A **plow** is used to cut and turn over the ground so that seeds can be planted.

The farmer will **plow** his land this spring.

We like to watch the farmer when he is **plowing.**

---

plum A **plum** is a **fruit.** Plums grow on a plum tree. There are red plums, purple plums and yellow plums.

---

pocket

Charlie Brown reaches into the **pocket** of his jacket. He put a note in his pocket so he wouldn't lose it. He is carrying his money in the pocket of his pants. A pocket is a part of our clothes in which we can put things.

---

pocketbook A **pocketbook** is a **purse.** Mother keeps money in her pocketbook.

---

poem A **poem** is a special way of telling us something. Poems are often very beautiful, and some tell us little stories. One poem that everyone likes begins this way:

'Twas the night before Christmas,
when all through the house
Not a creature was stirring—
not even a mouse.'

point "Could you please **point** out Charlie Brown's house to me?" asks Franklin. "Will you please **show** me which house is Charlie Brown's?"

Lucy **points** with her finger toward a white house. She sticks out her finger to show a white house. "It's over there," she says.

"Where?" asks Franklin.

"There! Look where I'm **pointing,**" Lucy says.

She **pointed** again to Charlie Brown's house.

My pencil has a **point.** My pencil has a **sharp end.**

---

poison Anything that is a **poison** will make you very sick if you eat it. Never put poison in your mouth.

pole

Woodstock is sitting on Snoopy's fishing **pole.** A pole is **a long stick** that is used for something. A flag waves from a flagpole. A telephone pole holds up telephone wires.

---

policeman A **policeman** helps me cross the street on my way to school. A policeman protects people. **Policemen** usually wear blue uniforms. Some policemen guard the streets. Some policemen ride in cars. Other policemen ride horses.

polite Frieda is **polite.**
Frieda is **kind and thoughtful of others.**
She says "Please" and "Thank you."

---

pond A **pond** is a **small lake.** Fish swim in the water of a pond. Some plants grow in it.

---

pony A **pony** is a **small horse.** I saw many **ponies** at the circus.

---

pool Linus was splashing in his wading **pool** when Snoopy popped out of the water and scared him. A pool holds water for swimmers and waders. Some pools are in the ground. Some pools are made of rubber and are placed on the ground.

The big children swim in a big swimming pool. The rain left little **pools** of water in the street.

poor The woman in the story was **poor.** She didn't have good clothes or good food. She didn't have much money.

We feel sorry for Baby when she falls down. We say, "Poor Baby."

Lucy did **poor** work in school because her eyes hurt.
Lucy did **bad** work in school because her eyes hurt.

---

porch Peppermint Patty and Snoopy are standing on the **porch** of her house. A porch is a little room or hall that is attached to the outside of the house. Patty's porch is small. Some porches are large and have tables and chairs on them. We sit on our porch in the summer.

post 

A **post** is a **thick stick** that stands straight up from the ground. In this game, the ball was supposed to hit the post, but Woodstock got in the way. Next time you want to sit on a post, Woodstock, sit on a fence post or a sign post.

---

postcard When I was away, I wrote to my friend on a **postcard.** I sent the postcard by mail.

---

postman The **postman** brings our letters to our house. Our postman is our **mailman.**

---

pot We cook our food in a metal **pot.** We make tea in a tea pot. A pot is like a bowl, but has a handle.

---

potato A **potato** is a **vegetable. Potatoes** are white with a brown skin. Sweet potatoes are yellow or orange. Potatoes grow in the ground. We had potatoes for dinner.

---

pound A **pound** is a measure of weight. My mother went to the store and bought a pound of sugar, a pound of coffee and a pound of butter.

Linus weighs sixty **pounds.**

Father will **pound** the nail with a hammer.
Father will **hit** the nail with a hammer.

He is **pounding** the nail into the wall.

pour Linus is careful to **pour** the milk from the bottle into the glass without getting milk on the table. He **pours** the milk until the glass is full. When you pour, you put liquid from one place to another.

He **poured** all the milk out of the bottle.

---

powder Mother is putting face **powder** on her face. Flour is a fine powder. We powder the baby to keep him cool after his bath.

---

pray

Linus kneels by his bed to **pray.**
He **prays** to God to take care of him.
He **asks** God to keep him safe.

---

prayer God will hear your **prayer.**
God will hear **what you say when you pray.**

---

present All the children were **present** except one.
All the children were **there** except one.

Daddy gave me a set of paints for a Christmas **present.**
Daddy gave me a set of paints for a Christmas **gift.**
There were many **presents** under the Christmas tree.

---

president The **President** of the United States of America is chosen by the people.
The **leader** of the United States of America is chosen by the people.
The president of our club is chosen by us.

press Mother will **press** her dress.
Mother will **iron** her dress.

I **press** the door shut gently.
I **push** the door shut gently.

I **pressed** the lid of the box down.

---

pretend

Snoopy wants to **pretend** that he is someone else.
He **pretends** that he is a cow.
He **makes believe** he is a cow.

---

pretty "Do you think I'm **pretty,** Schroeder?" asks Lucy.
"Do you think I'm **nice to look at?"**

---

price The **price** of the paper is five cents.
The **money it takes to buy** the paper is five cents.

---

prince The son of a king is a **prince.**

---

princess The daughter of a king is a **princess.**

prize Lucy won a race and was given a **prize.** The prize goes to the one who does something best.

---

promise I **promise** to go.
I **say** that I will go, and I will do as I say.

When I make a **promise** to my mother I always keep it.

I **promised** to take my little sister to the park

---

proper Winter is the **proper** season to wear a warm coat.
Winter is the **right** season to wear a warm coat.

It is proper to say "Thank you" when someone gives you something.

---

protect The children are playing ice hockey. They **protect** their hands with hockey gloves. They wear the gloves to **keep** their hands **from getting hurt.**

Each player **protects** the others on his team.
Each one on the team **takes care of** the other.

---

proud My father was **proud** of me when I won the race.
My father was **pleased** with me when I won the race.

pudding We eat **pudding** for dessert. Sometimes we have rice pudding. Sometimes we have chocolate pudding. We have plum pudding for Christmas dinner.

---

puff Sally puts powder on her face with a powder **puff.**

Linus blew the candles out with one **puff.**
Linus blew the candles out with one **quick, hard breath.**

The engine went "**Puff, puff,**" as it climbed the hill.

The big bad wolf said to the little pig, "I'll huff and I'll puff and I'll blow your house in."
So he huffed and he **puffed** and he blew the house in.

---

pull When you **pull** something, you **try to move it toward you.** Charlie Brown likes to pull the sled when Sally rides. Baby tries to pull my hair.

The horses **pulled** the wagon up the hill.

---

pumpkin Linus and Sally want an orange **pumpkin** for Halloween. They pick a big one off a vine. When they dig out the inside of the fruit, Linus's mother will use it to make a pumpkin pie.

puppy A **puppy** is a **baby dog.** Our dog had three **puppies.**

---

purple **Purple** is a **color.** You can make purple by mixing red and blue. Plums and grapes are often purple.

---

purse Mother carries a **purse** when she goes out. She keeps money and small things in her purse. **Pocketbook** is another name for purse.

---

push Snoopy gave Linus a **push** and Linus fell off the roof. "I saw you **push** Linus, Snoopy," said Lucy. "I saw you **shove** him."

Snoopy knows he should not have **pushed** Linus. He should not have pressed his paws against Linus **to make him move.**

---

put I **put** the ball on the table.
I **set** the ball on the table.

The boys **put up** a tent.
The boys **set up** a tent.

---

puzzle My sister got a jigsaw **puzzle** for her birthday. It was a picture cut into many pieces. We fitted the pieces together to make the picture again.

Did you ever tell a riddle? That is a puzzle with words.

quack "**Quack, quack,**" says the duck.

quarrel When children **quarrel,** they have a **fight with words.**

quart Linus drinks a **quart** of milk each day.
He drinks **four glasses** of milk each day.

quarter When you divide anything into four equal parts, you call each part a **quarter.** A quarter of an apple is **one-fourth** of an apple.

A **quarter** is **money.** A quarter is equal to **twenty-five cents** or five nickels. Four quarters make a dollar.

---

queen A **queen** is the **female ruler of a country. The wife of a king** is called a queen.

---

question When I want to find out something, I ask a **question.** I asked my mother a question. I said, "Where is my doll?" My mother answered my question. She said, "You left your doll on the porch."

This is a question mark: **?**

---

queer A dragon is a **queer-**looking animal.
A dragon is a **strange-**looking animal.

The cat's paws are **queer.**
The cat's paws are **different from most.**

---

quick Kitty is **quick.**
Kitty is **fast.**

---

quiet The children stopped talking and were **quiet.** They **made no noise.**
The children stopped running and were **quiet.**
They did **not move.**

quietly They walked downstairs **quietly.**
They walked downstairs **without making a noise.**

We sat **quietly.**
We sat **without moving.**

---

quit He **quit** playing because he was tired.
He **stopped** playing because he was tired.

---

quite I am **quite** happy.
I am **really** happy.

The shoe was **not quite** large enough.
The shoe was **almost** large enough.

R r

rabbit A **rabbit** is an **animal.** It jumps and runs very fast. Two rabbits are eating our carrots.

---

race The two boys ran a **race** to the corner. They wanted to see which one would get there first. In a race we find out which person is fastest.

---

radio Daddy turns on the **radio** to hear music and the news. The sounds we hear on the radio come through the air without wires.

---

radish A **radish** is a **vegetable.** The part of the radish that we eat is the root. We buy radishes in a bunch. We grow radishes in our garden.

---

rag The teacher is cleaning the blackboard with a **rag.**
The teacher is cleaning the blackboard with a **small cloth.**

The scarecrow's clothes were in **rags.**
The scarecrow's clothes were **torn and worn out.**

rail There was a metal **rail** across the gate.
There was a metal **bar** between the posts of the gate.

A train runs on **rails.**
A train runs on **bars of iron** laid on the ground.

---

railroad A **railroad** is a **road made of rails.** Trains run on the railroad.

---

rain Lucy and Linus are standing in the **rain.**
Drops of water are falling from the sky.

It **rains** often in the spring.
It **rained** yesterday.
It has been **raining** all day today.

---

rainbow When the sun starts to come out after it rains, we often see a **rainbow** in the sky. It looks like part of a circle and it has seven colors.
A rainbow lasts only a few minutes.

raise Lucy will **raise** her hand.
Lucy will **put up** her hand.

Did you ever take care of rabbits and **help** them **grow** up properly?
My mother won't let me **raise** rabbits, but I have a kitten.

---

rake I **rake** the leaves in the yard.
I **gather together** the leaves in the yard **with a rake.**

---

ranch Cows, horses or sheep are raised on a **ranch.**
Vegetables, grains or fruits are grown on a farm.
Would you rather live on a ranch or a farm?

---

rap I heard someone **rap** on the door.
I heard someone **knock** on the door. Someone **hit** the door **lightly with his hand.**

---

rat A **rat** is a small **animal.** It is like a mouse, but bigger.
Rats can be brown, black or white.

---

rather I would **rather** have milk than cocoa. I like it better.
I would rather play house than jump rope.
It is more fun.

---

raw The apple I ate was **raw.**
The apple I ate was **not cooked.** Some animals eat raw meat.
People eat cooked meat.

razor Daddy shaves his face with a **razor.**

---

reach

Linus must crawl under the table to **reach** the ball.
He tries to **touch** the ball **by stretching out his arm.**

Try **reaching** a little farther, Linus.
Good. You **reached** it.

---

read Charlie Brown can **read.**
He can look at words and tell what they mean.

He is **reading** a book.
He has **read** half of it already. He learned how to read at school.

---

ready Are we **ready** to go to the picnic? Yes, we have everything we need and everyone is here.

Now I am **ready** to go to bed.
Now **I feel like** going to bed. I have finished my story.

Marcie is **ready** for school. She had **done all that must be done** before she leaves. Her friend is not ready. Her friend still has things to do. She must put on her hat and coat before she can leave.

---

real The happenings we read about in the newspaper are **real.** The happenings we read about in a fairy story are not real.

---

really I **really** want to be a fireman when I grow up. I'm not fooling you. It's true.

---

reason What is the **reason** for going to town? Will you tell me **why** we are going to town?

---

receive

"Oh, how I like to **receive** letters," says Snoopy. Woodstock gives him an envelope and Snoopy takes it.

This is the first letter Snoopy has ever **received.**

---

recess When work stops, we have a **recess.** Children play at recess.

red **Red** is a **color.**
Charlie Brown is wearing a red shirt.

---

reindeer A **reindeer** is an **animal** that has long legs and big horns. Eight reindeer pull Santa Claus's sled.

---

remain I will **remain** at home until you call for me.
I will **stay** at home until you call for me.

---

remember I will **remember** your name.
I will **keep** your name **in my mind.**
I will **not forget** your name.

---

reply "Are you ready for school, Lucy?" Lucy's **reply** is "NO!"

Lucy should not **reply** that way. That's no way to **answer** a friendly question.

rest Snoopy is tired. He must **rest.**
He must stop what he is
doing and remain still
for a little while.

He wonders, "What shall I do for the **rest** of the day?"
"What shall I do for the **part** of the day **that is left?**"

---

return I will **return** your ball.
I will **give back** your ball.

Peppermint Patty has gone to see her aunt.
She will **return** tomorrow.
She will **come back** tomorrow.

I **returned** my book to the library.

---

ribbon I tie my hair back with a **ribbon.** The ribbon is blue to match my dress. I saved all the **ribbons** from my Christmas presents.

---

rice **Rice** is a **grain.** We buy rice at the grocery store. Rice grows in a field. Sometimes we have cooked rice to eat at supper.

---

rich The king is **rich.**
The king has **much money.**

riddle A **riddle** is a word puzzle. Can you guess this riddle?

Higher than a house, higher than a tree.
Oh! whatever can that be?

(Answer: a star)

---

ride You can **ride** in an automobile or a train. You can ride a bicycle. To ride is to be **carried along.**

ridden The horse was **ridden** until he was tired.

riding My big brother is **riding** in an automobile.

rode I **rode** downtown on a bus yesterday.

---

right Linus has a snowball in his **right** hand ready to throw at Lucy. It's not in his left hand.

"Don't do that, Linus. It's **not right** to throw things at your sister. It's **not a good thing** to do."

"Am I **right** or am I wrong," asks Linus, "that you threw one at me before?
"You're right," replies Lucy, "I did."

And with that, he throws the snowball right at Lucy. He throws it directly at Lucy—and it hits her.

---

ring

Schroeder heard the telephone **ring.** It **rang** and rang. Finally Schroeder answered. It was Lucy.
"Didn't you hear the telephone **ringing?**" she asked.
"It must have **rung** a hundred times."

Mother wears a wedding **ring** on her finger. It is a **circle** of gold.

The teacher said, "Stand in a **ring.**"
"Stand in a **circle.**"

ripe We pick fruit when it is **ripe.**
We pick fruit when it is **ready to eat.** One apple is ripe. The other apples are green.

rise What time will the sun **rise?**
What time will the sun **come up?**

I must **rise** from my chair.
I must **get up** from my chair.

The cake in the oven has **risen.**
Daddy **rose** when the lady came into the room.

river Snoopy is swimming in the **river.** A river is water that runs between two banks. A river is larger than a stream.

road We drove along the **road.** This road goes to the city. A **road** is a path for cars.

---

roar In winter I like to listen to the **roar** of the wind.
In winter I like to listen to the **loud sound** of the wind.

The lion can **roar.**
The lion can **make a loud noise.**

---

roast We are having a **roast** chicken for dinner tonight.
Mother **roasts** the meat in the oven to cook it.

---

rob To **rob** means to **steal** or take something away from another person.

---

robber A **robber** stole some money from the bank downtown.

---

robin A **robin** is a pretty **bird** with red feathers under its neck.

---

rock

Snoopy is sitting on a **rock.**
He is sitting on a **big stone.**

Mother **rocks** the baby to sleep. She sings "Rock-a-bye, baby."

roll

Linus is trying to **roll** a big snowball toward Snoopy's house. If he could get to a hill, the snowball would **turn over and over** by itself.

At night I **roll** myself up in a blanket. I **wrap** the blanket around myself.

I ate a **roll** for breakfast. A roll is a small cake of bread.

I **rolled** the string into a ball. I **wrapped** the string **around** itself until it looked like a ball.

---

roller skates

I like to skate on **roller skates.** The little wheels turn around and around as I go along.

---

roof

Snoopy likes to sleep on the **roof** of his doghouse. He likes to lie on the **top of his house.** A roof is the covering of a building.

room This is Lucy's **room.**
It's the place where her bed is and where she keeps all her things. There are six other rooms in her house.

Is there **room** for me in the car, or is it full?
Is there **a place** for me in the car?

rooster A **rooster** is a **father chicken.** On a farm, you hear the sound of a rooster early in the morning.

---

root A **root** is the **part of a plant below the ground.** Some plants have many roots.

---

rope

Snoopy has a **rope** around his neck. A rope is a kind of string that is very strong and thick.

---

rose A **rose** is a lovely **flower** that grows on a bush. Some roses climb over the wall or fence. We have pink, white, red and yellow roses in our garden.

rough The boys were very **rough** getting on the bus. They pushed and shoved and hurt each other.
They were **not gentle.**

The road was **rough.**
It was **very bumpy.** It was **not smooth.**

---

round A circle is **round.** A ball is round. Anything shaped like a ball or a circle is round.

row Baby put the blocks in a **row.**
Baby put the blocks in a **line.**

The sailor will **row** the boat.
He will use paddles to make the boat move.

Daddy **rowed** us across the lake in a boat.

---

rub Patty must **rub** the window with a rag to get the dirt off.

Mother **rubs** my back when it aches.

---

rubber Linus has lost one **rubber.** He will get his foot wet. He wears his **rubbers** over his shoes. They keep his feet dry.

I put a rubber band around my papers. I have rubber heels on my shoes. An automobile tire is made of rubber.

---

rude

Lucy was very **rude** to Linus.
She yelled at him. She was **not nice** to him.

---

rug Lucy has a **rug** beside her bed. She does not have to step on the bare floor when she gets up. A rug is a covering for the floor.

rule My mother has made a **rule** that I must be in bed by eight o'clock.

When you play games, you have **rules** to play by. The rules tell you what to do and what not to do.

---

ruler A **ruler** is a **stick for measuring** how long a thing is.

A **king** is a **ruler.** He rules over his people.

run See the children **run.**
They are **moving as fast as their feet can go.**

Where could they be **running** to?
They **ran** this way yesterday too.

---

rush My friend is in a **rush.**
He's in a big **hurry.**

He is late so he has **to rush.**
He is late and must **go quickly.**

S s

sad

Poor Linus. He's **sad** today.
He is **unhappy.**

saddle We put the **saddle** on the horse's back. A saddle is a **leather seat** for the person who rides the horse.

safe I am **safe** in my own house. Nothing bad can happen to me.
The policeman takes me across the street. I am safe from the cars.
I am **not in danger** from them.

sail There is a **sail** on the boat. A sail is like a large sheet. The boat moves fast when the wind blows hard.

A sailboat will not **sail** unless the wind blows.
A sailboat will not **move on the water** unless the wind blows. But a boat with an engine can sail without wind.

The big ship is **sailing** out to sea.

sailor A **sailor** works on a ship. He can sail a boat. There are many sailors in our navy.

sale We saw a house that was for **sale.** The people that owned it wanted to sell it.

---

salt I put **salt** on my egg. Food tastes better with salt in it. Sea water has salt in it. Most of the salt we eat comes from under the ground.

---

same Linus found three little birds that were all the **same.** They were **just alike.**

He looked for them the next day in the **same** place, but they were gone.

---

sand

Sally and Charlie Brown are playing in the **sand.** Sand is made up of very tiny pieces of rock. It feels like rough powder.

---

sandwich Lucy is making a **sandwich** for lunch. She puts meat and lettuce between two pieces of buttered bread.
Charlie Brown eats peanut butter **sandwiches** every day for his lunch.

Santa Claus **Santa Claus** comes at Christmas time
To make all children merry.
His beard is white, his smile is bright,
And his nose is red as a cherry.

In some countries, Santa Claus is called Saint Nicholas.

Saturday **Saturday** is the seventh **day** of the week.
Children do not go to school on Saturday.

---

saucer A **saucer** holds a cup for Daddy's coffee. A saucer holds milk for the kitty. I put cups and saucers on the table. A saucer is a small dish.

---

save I **save** part of my money.
I **do not spend** part of my money. I put it in my bank.

---

saw A **saw** cuts wood. The edge of a saw has small, sharp teeth.

Watch me **saw** the board.
Watch me **cut** the board with a saw.

---

say When I **say** something, I **speak** it.

I want to **say** something to you.
I want to **tell** you something.

Mother **says,** "Dinner's ready."
"What are you **saying?** Please speak louder."
"I **said,** I'm coming right away."

---

scare Snoopy tried to give Lucy **a scare.**
He tried to give her **a scared feeling.**

But it isn't easy **to scare** Lucy.
It takes more than a growl **to make** her **afraid.**

She isn't **scared** of Snoopy.
She isn't **afraid** of him.

scarecrow A **scarecrow** is made of sticks and dressed like a man. It is put in the field to scare the crows away.

---

school In **school** we learn to read and to write. We draw and paint pictures in school. We go to school early in the morning.

---

schoolhouse Charlie Brown is running out of the **schoolhouse.**
He's running away from the **building where he goes to school.**
School is over for the day.

schoolroom Our **schoolroom** has desks and blackboards in it. We learn our lessons in the schoolroom.

---

scissors I cut paper with **scissors.** My scissors have round ends. Mother cuts thread and cloth with scissors. Her scissors have sharp points. Mother uses the tiny scissors to trim her fingernails.

---

scold I do not like to have my sister **scold** me. I do not like to have my sister **say mean words** to me.

scooter I will take a ride on my **scooter.** It has two wheels. I put one foot on my scooter and push the ground with the other foot to make the scooter go.

---

scrap

Linus is showing his friends a **scrap** of cloth. It is a **small piece of cloth,** but it must be important to him.

---

scrape I must **scrape** the mud off my shoes before I go inside. I must **rub off** the mud.

---

scratch I have a **scratch** on my knee.
I have a **little cut** on my knee.

Did you see the cat **scratch** my hand with his claws?
Did you see the cat **make little cuts** in my hand with his claws?

Linus **scratched** himself on a nail.

---

scream Lucy and Charlie Brown heard a **scream.**
The **loud cry** came from Linus.

"What's making him **scream?**" asked Charlie Brown.
"Why are you **screaming?**" asked Lucy.
Linus **screamed** again and ran home.

scrub Cinderella must **scrub** the floor to make it clean.
Cinderella must **wash and rub** the floor **to make it clean.**

---

sea The **sea** is salt water and covers most of the earth. It is sometimes called the **ocean.** Ships travel on the sea. Fish swim in the sea.

---

season Summer is a **season.** The four seasons of the year are spring, summer, autumn and winter. Which of the four seasons do you like best?

---

seat The bus driver is not in his **seat.**
Only his hat is on the **chair.**
Snoopy would like to sit in the driver's seat.

second

Charlie Brown is first in line. Snoopy is **second.** Franklin is third.

A **second** is a **measure of time.** It is very short. There are sixty seconds in a minute.

---

secret I know a **secret.**
I know **something that no one else knows.**

Something that is hidden is secret. We have a secret hiding place.

---

see I **see** with my eyes. Do you see Violet hiding behind the chair? I see her.

I don't **see** why Lucy is so angry today.
I don't **know** why Lucy is so angry today.

Tomorrow I am going to the farm to **see** my aunt.
Tomorrow I am going to the farm to **visit** my aunt.

saw We **saw** a parade yesterday.
seen I have not **seen** my aunt for a long time.

---

seed Almost every plant grows from a **seed.** There are seeds that we plant in the vegetable garden to grow corn, peas and carrots. The seeds are covered with earth. We plant flower seeds too.

seem Does this answer **seem** right to you?
Does this answer **look** right to you?

Feel my face. Does it **seem** hot to you?
Does it **feel** hot to you?

Does this candy **seem** too sweet?
Does this candy **taste** too sweet?

The policeman **seemed** to be a strong man.
My mother **seems** to be in a hurry.

---

seesaw Sally and Linus are playing on the **seesaw.** One end of the seesaw goes up while the other end goes down.

---

sell The man will **sell** you a balloon.
The man will **give** you a balloon **for money.**

The man is **selling** balloons.
He **sold** me a balloon.

---

send Who would **send** a letter to a dog?
Who would **have someone take** a letter to Snoopy?

Charlie Brown must have **sent** it.
He must have **mailed** it to Snoopy from camp

I am **sending** you a picture.

Mother **sent** me upstairs.
Mother **made me** go upstairs.

---

sense Daddy has good **sense.** He knows the right thing to do.

I have a **sense** of taste. I also have a sense of touch, of hearing, of seeing and of smelling These are my five **senses.**

September **September** is the ninth **month** of the year. It has thirty days. It comes in the autumn. We go back to school in September after our summer vacation.

---

serve Here comes Lucy to **serve** Snoopy his dinner. She brings his dish to the place where he eats.

"I love being **served** by a beautiful girl," thinks Snoopy.

A good American will **serve** his country.

A good American will **help and work** for his country.

---

set

Snoopy has a **set** of books. He has a **group** of books **that belong together.**

Violet can **set** the table. She can **put** the dishes and silver on it

Let me **set** the chair over here.
Let me **put** the chair over here.

---

seven **Seven** is a number that looks like this: **7.** Let's count to seven: 1 2 3 4 5 6 **7.**

---

several **Several** butterflies are following Snoopy.
There are **more than a few** butterflies, but there are not many. There are about five or six or maybe eight butterflies with Snoopy.

sew We **sew** with a needle and thread. I will sew a dress for my doll.

I **sewed** many dresses for my dolls.
I am **sewing** with black thread.

---

shade Let's sit in the **shade** of this tree.
Let's sit in the **shadow** of this tree. It's cooler in the shade than in the sun.

My umbrella will **shade** me from the sun.
It will **keep the sun off** me.

A window shade can be raised to let sunlight into a room, or pulled down to keep out the light.

---

shadow When the sun shines in front of me I can see my **shadow** on the ground behind me.
I can see a shade that's the same shape as my body.

My shadow does everything I do. It follows me wherever I go.

---

shake Friends **shake** hands when they meet.
They **take hold** of each other's hands **and move** them **up and down quickly.**

Snoopy and Peppermint Patty are **shaking** hands.

shook Linus **shook** the tree to get Snoopy to come down.
He **moved** the tree **back and forth quickly.**

shall I **shall** be happy when summer comes.
I **will** be happy when summer comes.

---

shape The **shape** of a box is square. The shape of a ball is round.

---

share The boys picked a pail of berries. Each boy took his **share.** Each boy took his **part.**

Lucy and Charlie Brown will **share** the candy.
Lucy and Charlie Brown with **each have a part** of the candy.

---

sharp The butcher has a **sharp** knife. It cuts the meat easily. My mother has sharp scissors. They cut the cloth easily. Pins and needles have sharp points.

---

shave To **shave** means to **cut off hair with a razor.**

Father is **shaving** his face.

---

she Sally is my sister. I think **she** is a nice girl.

---

shed At the side of the barn is a low building. It is a **shed.** The farmer keeps his wood in it. It is a wood shed.

---

sheep A **sheep** is a gentle **animal.** The body of a sheep is covered with wool. **Many sheep** together are a flock of sheep.

---

sheet Mother puts a clean **sheet** on my bed. The sheet keeps the blankets from touching me.
May I have a **sheet** of paper? May I have a **piece** of paper?

shelf The clock is on the top **shelf** of the cupboard. **Shelves** are boards that hold things.

shell An egg **shell** is the **hard outside** of an egg. A nut shell is the hard outside of a nut. Mother breaks the egg shell before she puts the egg in the cake.

I found a seashell near the water.
A sort of fish once lived inside it.

shine To **shine** means **to send out light.** The lights of the city shine at night. The sun shines in the daytime.

The moon **shone** last night.

shiny Linus has **shiny** gold buttons on his sailor coat.
Linus has **bright** gold buttons on his sailor coat.

ship A **ship** sails on the water.
A **very big boat** sails on the water. The ships sail on the ocean to all parts of the world.

shirt Charlie Brown's **shirt** is black and yellow. He wears a shirt on the upper part of his body.

shoe I have a hole in my **shoe.** My sock shows through the hole.

I must get a new pair of **shoes. Shoes** are **coverings for feet.**

---

shoot The men **shoot** at the wild ducks with their guns. They are trying to hit the ducks.

Linus is **shooting** his arrows at the tree. My father **shot** some rabbits on his hunting trip.

---

shop **A place where things are sold** is sometimes called a **shop.** Mother went to the shop to buy food. The shop was a grocery **store.**

A place where things are made or mended is sometimes called a shop. Charlie Brown took his bicycle to the shop to be fixed. My mother took me to a shop where shoes are made.

Mother and I went downtown **to shop** for new clothes. Mother and I went downtown **to look at and buy** new clothes.

We have been **shopping** all afternoon.

---

shore The **land at the edge of a body of water** is called the **shore.** We stood on the shore of Lake Erie and looked at the ships on the water.

---

short Peppermint Patty is too **short** to reach the top of the desk.

She is **not tall** enough to reach.

In a **short time** we will go back to school. It is **not a long time** before we go back to school.

shoulder

Charlie Brown carries his bat on his **shoulder.**

You have two **shoulders.** Your arms are attached to your shoulders.

---

shout Linus and Lucy heard Charlie Brown **shout,** "Hurray!" He **called out loudly** so they would be sure to hear him.

He was very happy.
He **shouted** with joy.
He was still **shouting**
when he ran past them.

---

shovel Charlie Brown is digging up the ground with his **shovel.** His shovel has a long handle at the end of a big flat spoon that breaks the dirt and can be used to lift it.

Daddy uses a coal shovel to lift coal into the furnace.
We shovel snow with a snow shovel. What do you use to shovel sand into your pail?

show "**Show** me what you have there," said Charlie Brown to Linus. **"Let** me **see** what you have."

Linus **showed** him a letter.
"I wouldn't go **showing** that around if I were you," said Charlie Brown.

Can you show me the way to school?
Please show me how this toy works.

We saw a **show** on television. The actors sang and danced and told funny stories.

---

shower A **shower** of water came from the hose.

We got caught in a **shower.**
We got caught in a **light rain.**

I am taking a shower bath to wash myself clean.

---

shut Please **shut** the window. Please **close** the window.

---

sick Linus is **sick.**
He is **not well.** He has a stomach ache. Charlie Brown will stay with him until the doctor comes. The doctor will make Linus well.

---

side One **side** of the clown's suit is red. One **part** is red.

Which **side** do you want to play on?
Which **team** do you want to play with?

We crossed the street to the other side.

sidewalk Lucy and Sally are walking on the **sidewalk.** The sidewalk is at the side of the street. People walk on the sidewalk. Cars, buses and trucks run in the street.

sight A man must have good **sight** to drive a car.
He must see well.

The airplane went behind the clouds **out of sight.**
It could **not** be **seen.**

Pig-Pen was all dirty. His mother said, "He's a **sight!**"
His mother said, "He's a **thing to see!**"

---

sign A **sign** tells us something important.
Charlie Brown sees a **sign** that says "Bus Stop." This sign tells him that this is the place on the street where the bus stops so that people can get on or off it.

A street sign tells you the name of the street.

A road sign may tell the driver that there is danger ahead.

I **sign** my name on my school papers.
I **write** my name on my papers.

---

signal The policeman gave the **signal** for the children to cross the street.
He blew a whistle and waved his arm.

Thunder is a signal that it's going to rain.

---

silent We were **silent** while Violet sang. We did **not speak.**

Falling snow is **silent.**
Falling snow **makes no noise.**

---

silk **Silk** cloth is made from very soft and fine threads.
The silk threads are made by silkworms.

silly My kitten is acting **silly.** He is chasing his tail. To be silly is to do funny things.

---

silver The dishes and the spoon are made of **silver.** My knife and fork are made of silver. Some money is made from silver. Silver is a **metal.**

---

since I have not been to visit Grandmother **since** Christmas. I have not been to visit Grandmother **from that time until now.**

---

sing Linus does not **sing** very well, but he likes to **sing.** He likes **to make music with his voice.**

He **sings** loudly.
His **singing** sounds funny.
He **sang** in school one day and everybody laughed.
He sang a song he had never **sung** before.

---

sink Sally is standing at the **sink.** She leans over the **big bowl** to brush her teeth.

A sink is a bowl with faucets.

I threw a rock in the water and watched it **sink.**
I threw a rock in the water and watched it **go down.**

The ship **sank** in the storm at sea.
The soap had **sunk** to the bottom of the bathtub.

sir To a man we sometimes say, "Yes, **sir,**" or "No, sir."
A soldier says, "Yes, sir," or "No, sir," when he speaks to his captain.

sister Sally is Charlie Brown's **sister.** Sally and Charlie Brown have the same father and mother.

sit

Lucy likes **to sit** on the floor to watch television.

Linus **sat** with her for a while.
Then he got tired of **sitting** so he stood up and left.

six **Six** is the number that comes after five. Let's count to **6:**
1 2 3 4 5 6.

size **Size** means **how big** or **how little.**
Charlie Brown and Schroeder are the same size.

skate

Linus can **skate** fast.
He is a good **skater** and likes to go **skating** on the ice.
Yesterday he **skated** for three hours.
You wear **skates** on your feet to roll or slide.

skin The covering of your body is your **skin.** When you take a bath, you wash your skin all over.

The covering of animals and plants is the skin. You peel the skin from a banana before you eat it.

---

skip Snoopy is a dog who can **skip** rope.
He can **jump** rope just like the girls.

He is **skipping** rope with Violet.

I **skipped** lunch today.
I **missed** having lunch.

skirt Patty gave Violet a pink **skirt** to wear with sweaters. A skirt is **a piece of clothing that hangs from the waist.** The skirt of a dress is the part that hangs below the waist.

---

sky You can see stars in the **sky** above you at night. You can see the sun in the sky in the daytime. Sometimes there are clouds in the sky.

---

slap When a mosquito bites me, I **slap** it.
When a mosquito bites me, I **hit it with my open hand.**

---

sled I have a new **sled.** I sit on my sled and Daddy pulls me through the snow.

---

sleep If I don't get enough **sleep,** I feel tired.
When you **sleep,** you are **not awake.**
Baby has **to sleep** all night and part of the day.

When Baby is **sleeping,** he is quiet and peaceful.
He **slept** through all the noise.

---

sleepy

Snoopy is **sleepy.** Snoopy is tired. He is ready to go to sleep.

sleeve The **sleeve** of my coat covers my arm.

---

sleigh A **sleigh** is a big sled. Grandfather used to drive a sleigh when there was snow on the roads. Santa Claus has a sleigh pulled by reindeer.

---

slice I cut off a **slice** of bread. I cut off a **piece** of bread. I put jam and butter on it.

Mother will **slice** the cake.
Mother will **cut** the cake **into slices.**

---

slide Charlie Brown likes to **slide** on the ice. If he starts by running, then he can **move easily and smoothly** across the ice with his feet still.

One time he **slid** all the way across the pond.

---

slip Linus does not **slip** when he walks on the ice. But Snoopy **slips** every time. His **feet slide out from under** him and down he goes.

He tried to keep from **slipping** by walking slowly, but he **slipped** anyhow.

---

slipper A **slipper** is a light soft shoe. We wear **slippers** in the house.

slippery Ice is **slippery** to walk on.
A fish is slippery. It slides out of Mother's hands when she tries to hold it.

---

slow Charlie Brown is **slow.**
Charlie Brown is **not fast.** He will be late for school.

---

slowly The wagon moved **slowly** up the hill. It took a long time to go up the hill.

---

small The kitten is **small.** The cat is large.
The kitten is **little.**

The kitten is **smaller** than the cat.
The kitten is the **smallest** animal on our block.

---

smell Snoopy has a very strong sense of **smell.**
He can **tell with his nose** that his dinner is almost ready.

He **smelled** it cooking.

Roses have a nice **smell.**
I don't like the smell of onions.

smile

The big **smile** on Peppermint Patty's face shows that she is happy.
Lucy gave her something that made her smile.

---

smoke There is **smoke** coming from Snoopy's house. Something must be burning. Smoke is the **gray cloud that comes from a fire.**

Father **smokes** a pipe.
He **puffs** on the pipe.

smooth My table is **smooth** on top. There are no bumps in it.
It is **not rough.** Glass is smooth.
I use a comb and brush to smooth my hair.
I skated **smoothly** on the ice. I did not trip or fall.

---

snake A **snake** is a long thin **animal** without legs. A snake moves by crawling.

---

snap Mother's purse closes with a **snap.** Have you ever heard the snap of burning wood?

Can you **snap** your fingers? A snap is a short, sharp noise.

The dog will **snap** at the cat if she comes near his food.
The dog will **bite quickly** at the cat if she comes near his food.

snapped The turtle **snapped** at the stick.

---

sneeze I am catching cold. I **sneeze.** A **sneeze** sounds like this: "Kerchoo!"

---

snow Lucy and Charlie Brown are out in the **snow.** When rain freezes, it turns to snow
and falls softly from the sky.
Snow piles up and makes
everything white.

It started to **snow.**
It **snowed** all night.
It's still **snowing.**

snowball Linus has a **snowball.** He made the ball out of snow. It was almost round.

---

snowflake A **snowflake** is one small piece of snow that falls from the sky.
Some snowflakes look like flowers. Some look like stars.

---

snowman Linus made a **snowman** by rolling snow into three big balls and putting one on top of the other. He used stones for the eyes and buttons.

---

snowstorm Woodstock will find it hard to fly because there is a **snowstorm.** The snow is falling thick and fast. It's windy and hard to see. Snoopy thinks he'll have to come back.

so It was raining, **so** we wore our boots.
It was raining. **For that reason,** we wore our boots.

To have your picture taken, hold your head just **so.**
To have your picture taken, hold your head **just this way.**

I have been playing hard and I'm **so** tired.
I have been playing hard and I'm **very** tired

My mother says, "Is that **so?**"
She means, "Is that **true?**"

I am seven years old, and **so** is Lucy.
I am seven years old, and Lucy is **too.**

---

soap

Lucy is washing her hands with **soap** and water to make them clean. She rubs herself with **soap** to wash herself. Mother uses **soap flakes** to wash our clothes and dishes.

---

socks Snoopy is wearing **socks** on his feet to keep his feet warm. If he were a person, he would put shoes on over his socks.

soft A pillow is **soft.** A rock is hard. The kitten is soft to touch.

My mother speaks in a **soft** voice.
My mother speaks in a **low** voice.

---

soldier A **soldier** will fight for his country. A soldier is part of the army. The soldiers march. They wear uniforms.

---

some Pick out **some** girl to help you.
Pick out **a** girl to help you.

My brother gave me **some** pennies.
My brother gave me **several** pennies.

---

somebody I heard Mother say that **somebody** is coming to see us.
I heard Mother say that **some person** is coming to see us.

---

someone Is it **someone** we know?
Is is **some person** we know?

---

something There is **something** I cannot see behind that door.
There is **a thing** I cannot see behind that door.

---

sometime I am going to the library **sometime** soon.
I am going to the library **one time or another** soon.

sometimes Violet wears her hair in curls **sometimes.**
Violet wears her hair in curls **once in a while.**

---

somewhere The sun is shining **somewhere** at all times.
The sun is shining in **some place** at all times.

Are you going **somewhere?**
Are you going to **some place?**

---

son Linus is his father's **son.** He is also his mother's son.
A boy is the son of his mother and father.

---

song A **song** is made up of words and music that go together.
"Three Blind Mice" is a song.

---

soon Our class at school is going to have a picnic **soon.**
Our class at school is going to have a picnic **in a short time.**

---

sorry I was **sorry** when Snoopy hurt his paw. I felt **sad.**
I am sorry I did wrong. I wish I had been good.
I am sorry I cannot come to the party. I would like to come.

---

sound A train whistle makes a loud **sound.**
A train whistle makes a loud **noise.** A clock ticking makes little sound. We hear **sounds** with our ears.

Baby fell down, but Mother said he was safe and **sound.**
Baby fell down, but Mother said he was safe and **not hurt.**

soup Mother made some **soup** by boiling meat and vegetables in water.

---

sour Lemon juice tastes **sour.** We put sugar in it to make it sweet. Something sour does **not** taste **sweet** or fresh.
The milk turned sour because it was not kept cold.

---

south As you face the early morning sun, to your right is **south.** On a map, south is at the bottom.

---

spade The farmer is digging with a **spade.** A spade is a kind of **shovel.**

---

sparrow A **sparrow** is a little brown **bird.** We see more sparrows than any other kind of bird.

---

speak My cat cannot **speak,** but he makes a noise.
My cat cannot **say words,** but he makes a noise.

spoke Yesterday I **spoke** to my father over the telephone.

spoken My mother has **spoken** to me about keeping my bedroom neat.

---

special A **special** day is different from the other days. It is an **important** day. Your birthday is a **special** day.
When I was sick, mother made me a **special** dinner. The rest of the family ate something else.
Lucy is my **special** friend. I like her better than anyone else.
We play hockey with a special kind of stick. It is made just for hockey and is not like any other stick.

speed Snoopy is running at full **speed.**
He is running **as fast as he can.**

The electric fan has two speeds:
slow and fast.

I **sped** down the hill on my bike.
I **went as fast as I could.**

The man was stopped for **speeding** in his car.

---

spell

Charlie Brown can **spell** his name.
He can say the letters of his name in the right order.

---

spend I will **spend** five cents for candy.
I will **pay** five cents for candy.

I **spent** ten cents for a box of crayons last week.

---

spider A **spider** is a **bug** with eight legs. It spins a pretty web.

---

spill You **spill** water if you **let it run out** of a glass or pail.

You can also spill water if you **put more in the glass than the glass can hold.**

---

spin The top will **spin** when I pull the string.
The top will **turn around and around** when I pull the string.

splash Snoopy made Patty fall backward into the pool with a big **splash.**
Drops of water sprayed up like a fountain and sprinkled Snoopy.

"I'll **splash** you for that," she yelled.
"I'll **throw water** on you."

Patty **splashed** around trying to get up.
Snoopy left her still **splashing** in the pool.

---

spoil If you spill ink on your dress, you will **spoil** it. If you cook the meat too long, you will spoil it. To spoil something is to harm it.

I dropped my book in the mud and **spoiled** it.

He is a **spoiled** child.
He is a naughty child because he has been allowed to do everything he wants to.

spoon Lucy is eating her cereal with a **spoon.** We use a spoon to lift soft foods to our mouths when we eat.

---

spot Sally got a **spot** on her dress. The spot is **dirt.**

Pig-Pen made a **spot** on the paper with ink.
Pig-Pen made a **mark** on the paper with ink.

Is this the **spot** where the accident happened?
Is this the **place** where the accident happened?

---

spray Lucy has a **spray** can. When she pushes a small part of the can, a spray of water shoots out. A spray is a **stream of tiny drops.** Water **sprays** from a fountain or from a faucet. Lucy **sprayed** water on Schroeder to get his attention.

spread The dress is **spread** out to dry.
The dress is **opened** out **flat** to dry.

Our sandwiches were **spread** with jelly and peanut butter.
Our sandwiches were **covered** with jelly and peanut butter.

---

spring **Spring** is one of the four seasons of the year.
The others are summer, autumn and winter.

Spring up means **jump up.**

There are **springs** in my bed that make it easy to lie on.

---

sprinkle When it rains lightly, we say, "It's only a **sprinkle.**"

I like to **sprinkle** the lawn. I sprinkle water on my doll clothes before I iron them. I sprinkle bread crumbs on the snow for the birds to eat.

---

square Let's draw a **square** on the blackboard. A square has four sides. All sides of a square are the same.

---

squeeze We **squeeze** oranges to get the juice out of them.
We **press** oranges **hard** to get the juice out of them.

Sometimes when you say **squeeze,** you mean **hug.** I put my arms around Mother and squeeze her.

I **squeezed** the suitcase shut.
I **pressed hard** on the suitcase to shut it.

---

squirrel A **squirrel** is a small **animal** with a big, furry tail. A squirrel lives in the trees. He likes to eat nuts.

stable I keep my pony in a **stable.** He is fed in the stable. He sleeps in the stable. A stable is a building for animals.

---

stair

Peppermint Patty is walking down the **stairs.** A **stair** is **one step in a group of steps.** All of the steps are the **stairs.**

---

stamp A **stamp** is a little square of paper that we buy at the post office. We stick a stamp on a letter to pay for having it taken where we want it to go

When I am angry, I **stamp** my foot.
I **put** my foot **down hard.**
Mother **stamped** her feet to get the snow off.

---

stand Charlie Brown must **stand** to read to the class. He must **be on his feet** until he is finished. Then he may sit down.

Snoopy is not **standing.** He is sitting. Charlie Brown **stood** there for a long time.

His book was on a **stand.** A book stand keeps a book open so that you can read it easily.

---

star

A **star** makes a bright little light in the sky at night. Many stars are in the sky on a clear night. Many are really suns. They look small because they are very far away.

There are fifty **stars** in the American flag. There is one for each of the fifty states of the United States.

start The parade will **start** from the circus tent.
The parade will **begin** to move from the circus tent.

The ball game will start at three o'clock.
The ball game will begin at three o'clock.

The show **started** with music.

---

state We live in the **state** of Ohio. Uncle Raymond lives in the state of Texas. What state do you live in? There are fifty states in the United States of America.

---

station The children are at the bus **station.** The camp bus will stop for them. The bus stops at the station to pick up people and to let other people off.

The building in which fire trucks and fire engines are kept is called a fire station.
A train stops at a railroad station.
We stop our car at a gas station to get gas.

stay

Lucy plans to **stay** where she is. She will **not move.** She may be there for hours.

She is angry and wishes she had **stayed** at home.

---

steal To **steal** means to take something that does not belong to you.

A bad boy tried to steal my pail.

Yesterday he **stole** my shovel.
If my pail and shovel are **stolen,** I won't be able to play in the sand.

---

steam When water gets very hot, it boils and becomes **steam.** Watch the steam come out of the tea kettle. Some engines are run by steam. They are steam engines.

---

steep There is a **steep** hill near our house. The path on it goes almost straight up.

---

step Snoopy fell down one **step** after another. He hit every **stair** on his way down.

Watch your **step!**
Watch where you **put your foot when you walk.**

Step to the back of the bus.
Walk to the back of the bus.

I **stepped** around the puddle.

stick Charlie Brown is holding a **stick.**
He is holding a **long thin piece of wood.**

Don't **stick** your hand with the pin.
Don't **put the sharp point** of the pin in your hand.

Stick the stamp on the letter.
Fasten the stamp on the letter.

The car got **stuck** in the mud.

---

stiff My new shoes feel **stiff.** They **do not bend easily** when I walk.

---

still Snoopy had been barking. Then he became **still.**
He **didn't make any noise.**

He curled up and lay **still.**
He curled up and lay **without moving.**

Snoopy **still** hasn't moved.
Snoopy hasn't moved **up to now.**

---

sting Did a bee ever **sting** you? It feels as though you are being stuck with a pin.

Lucy was **stung** on the arm by a bee. Her arm hurt and swelled up.

---

stir I must **stir** the soup.
I must **move** the soup **round and round with my spoon.**

stocking Sally is going to hang up her **stocking.** Stockings are longer than socks. They cover our legs and feet.

Mother has a pair of black stockings.

---

stomach

Snoopy ran head first into Charlie Brown's **stomach.** He hit Charlie Brown right in the **middle of his body.**

When you swallow food, it goes down your throat into your stomach.

---

stone A **stone** is a **piece of rock.** Linus threw a stone into the air.

My mother's ring has a **stone** in it. The stone is a **diamond.**

---

stool A **chair without a back** is a **stool.** We use it in the kitchen to sit on. The farmer uses a stool to sit on while he milks the cows.

stop Charlie Brown is waiting for the bus to **stop.**
He is waiting for the bus to **arrive.**
He waited so long he fell asleep.

The red light on the street means **"Stop!"**
The red light on the street means **"Do not go any farther."**

"Please **stop** shouting," Mother said. **"Don't do it any more."**

I **stopped** my dog from following me down the street.
The light is red, so the cars are **stopping.**

store A **place where things are sold** is a **store.** We buy our food in a grocery store.

The farmer will **store** the corn for his pigs to eat during the winter.
The farmer will **put away** the corn for his pigs to eat during the winter.

In the summer, my mother **stores** my winter clothes in a closet.

---

storm

Lucy and Snoopy are out in a **storm.** The wind is blowing hard and the rain is pouring down. Sometimes thunder and lightning come with a storm.

The snow is falling thick and fast. We are having a snowstorm.

---

story Aunt Ellen is telling a **story.** The story is "The Three Bears."

---

stove Mother cooks on a **stove** in the kitchen. In some houses, there is a stove to warm the rooms.

---

straight I tried to draw a **straight** line.
I tried to draw a line with no bumps or bends in it.
But it came out a little bit crooked.

strange I will start tomorrow at a **strange** school. I have never been there before.

I will be in a class with strange children. I don't know any of them.

A dragon is a **strange-**looking animal.
A dragon is a **queer-**looking animal.

---

straw Linus is drinking through a **straw.** A straw is usually made of paper. It is hollow, and you can pull water through it with your breath.

The **dry, hollow stems** of the wheat plant that are left after the grains are taken are also called **straw.**

I have a straw hat.

---

stream Snoopy is crossing the **stream** by stepping on stones. A stream is **a little river.**

Something that moves in a straight, narrow line is sometimes called a stream.
A stream of cars sped by.
The light streamed in the window.

---

street A **street** is a **road in the city or town.** The street I live on is called Main Street. What is the name of your street? There are many streets in our town.

stretch "See how high I can **stretch.**" Linus is showing Charlie Brown how high he **can reach out his arms.**

I **stretch** a rubber band.
I **pull out** the rubber band so that it is longer.

Linus **stretched** to catch the ball.
I am **stretching** my sweater to make it bigger.

---

strike I saw Lucy **strike** her little brother.
I saw her **hit** him **hard.**

When you play baseball, you try to hit the ball with your baseball bat. If you **miss the ball** when you try to hit it, that is called a **strike.**
If you miss the ball three times, you have **struck out.**

When Lucy **struck** him, Linus fell on his head.
Striking someone is a dangerous thing to do.

---

string We use **string** to tie packages. When you buy string in the store, it is rolled into a ball.

---

strip My belt is made of a **strip** of leather.
My belt is made of a **narrow piece** of leather.

He will **strip** and jump into the water.
He will **take off his clothes** and jump into the water.

stripe A **stripe** is a narrow line of color with different colors on each side of it.
Daddy has a tie with red, blue and yellow stripes.
He has a blue and white striped shirt too.
Linus always wears a shirt with red and black **stripes.**

---

strong A **strong** man can lift heavy things. He is **not weak.**

When I read, I like a strong light so that I can see well.

Our big swing hangs from a strong rope.

Some kinds of cheese have a strong taste.

---

stuff Daddy said, "I don't need the **stuff** in that box."
Daddy said, "I don't need the **things** in that box."

When I make my bear, I will **stuff** it with cotton.
When I make my bear, I will **fill** it with cotton.

My bed pillow is **stuffed** with feathers.

---

such I have read several **such** books.
I have read several books **of that kind.**

He was **such** a big dog!
He was a **very** big dog!

sugar **Sugar** is made from a plant called sugar cane. It is also made from sugar beets. I sweeten my lemonade with sugar. There is sugar in candy. Sugar makes the candy sweet.

---

suit

Did you ever see a dog wearing a **suit?** Snoopy is wearing a **jacket and trousers that match.**

Charlie Brown and Sally are going swimming. They wear **bathing suits.**

This hat **suits me.**
This hat **looks good on me.**

I hope this book will **suit** you. I hope it will **please** you.

---

suitcase A **suitcase** is a **bag** used **for carrying clothes** when you travel. Snoopy also puts his dish in his suitcase when he goes on a trip.

---

summer The **summer** is one of the four **seasons** of the year. The other seasons are autumn, winter and spring. There is much sunshine in the summer. The sunshine makes summer a warm season.

---

sun

The **sun** shines in the daytime. It is bright and makes you warm.

Sunday **Sunday** is the first **day** of the week. Most people do not go to work on Sunday. Sunday is a day of rest. Many people go to church on Sunday.

---

sunshine The **light of the sun** is **sunshine.** Plants grow in the sunshine. Sunshine is good for children.

---

supper Sally is bringing Snoopy his **supper.**
We eat **supper** in the evening.
We have a **light dinner** in the evening.

---

suppose I **suppose** we should go.
I **think perhaps** we should go.

I **supposed** they would be late.
I **guessed** they would be late.

I'm **supposed** to go out today.
I **should** go out today.

Supposing we go tomorrow instead?
How would it be if we went tomorrow instead?

---

sure I am **sure** that I am eight years old. I am sure that I am a boy. I am sure that my name is Charlie Brown. I **know** all these things.

surprise

Snoopy got a **surprise.**
He got **something he did not expect.**

Snoopy was **surprised** that he caught the ball.
He **did not expect** to catch it.

---

surround Many trees **surround** our house.
They are **all around** our house.

An island is **surrounded** by water.
There are flowers **surrounding** the pond.

---

swallow When I eat, I chew my food, then I **swallow** it.
It goes down my throat into my stomach.

---

sweater

Charlie Brown has a new **sweater.**
He has a **short jacket made of yarn** to keep him warm.

sweep I **sweep** the floor.
I **brush** the floor **with a broom** to clean it.

Frieda was **sweeping** the leaves from the walk.
She has **swept** the walk clean.

---

sweet Sugar is **sweet.** Anything made with sugar is sweet. Candy is sweet. Honey is sweet too.

Mother says, "Baby is so sweet!"

---

swell To **swell** means to **grow bigger.** When I blow air into the balloon, it will swell. Linus pinched his finger in the door, and it began to swell.

Sometimes the children say, "That's **swell!**"
They mean, "That's **very good.**"

---

swift Peppermint Patty is a **swift** runner.
She is a **very fast** runner.

She is **swifter** than her friends.
She runs **swiftly.**

swim The girls can **swim** better than the boys.
They **glide** smoothly **through the water.**

They **swam** across the lake quickly.
The boys were **swimming** behind them.

The girls are good swimmers because they have **swum** more than the boys.

swing There is a **swing** in our yard.
I like to sit on it and **swing.**
I like to **move back and forth through the air.**

I saw a monkey **swinging** by his tail.
He **swung** from branch to branch.

T t

table The children are seated around the **table.** The table has a flat top held up by strong legs. They will eat their dinner at the table.

tag There was a **tag** on my Christmas present.
There was a **piece of card tied with a string** on my Christmas present.

There is a **game** called **tag.** One player runs after another until he touches him. Do you know how to play tag?

---

tail Dogs and many other animals have **tails.** Snoopy wags his **tail** when he is happy. Sometimes he sits on his tail.

---

take

Snoopy doesn't want Lucy to **take** his supper dish away.
He doesn't want her to **get hold of** it and **carry** it away.

Daddy will **take** us to the ball game.
Daddy will **go with us** to the ball game.

I will **take** a book from the shelf.
I will **get** a book from the shelf.

I will **take** five minutes to get ready.
I will **need** five minutes to get ready.

We **take** a bus to go downtown.
We **ride** on a bus to go downtown.

You **take** the stairs to the second floor.
You **walk** on the stairs to the second floor.

Take this package to Mother.
Carry this package to Mother.

Pig-Pen has **taken** one cookie.
Mother **takes** me to the show.
Linus is **taking** a ride on his sled.

took Violet **took** her books home with her.

---

tale Our kindergarten teacher told us the **tale** of "Little Red Riding Hood."
Our kindergarten teacher told the **story** of "Little Red Riding Hood."

---

talk Charlie Brown and Lucy are having a **talk.**
To **talk** means to **say words.** I can talk to my dog, but my dog cannot talk to me.

I **talked** to Daddy over the telephone.
I was **talking** about the animals I saw at the circus.

---

tall Linus is **not** very **tall.** He is **short.**

Violet is **taller** than he is.
Her head is above his.

Violet is **taller** than the snowman. She is the **tallest** of them all.

tame A **tame** animal is one that is not afraid of people. Dogs and cats and horses are tame animals. Lions and tigers are wild animals. Tame animals are usually **gentle.**

---

tan Charlie Brown wore tan shoes.
Charlie Brown wore **light brown** shoes.

Lucy played in the sun every day. She got a nice tan.

---

tap We heard a **tap** on the window.
We heard a **light knock** on the window.

Will you **tap** that boy on the shoulder?
Will you **touch** that boy on the shoulder?

---

tardy I must not be **tardy** to school.
I must not be **late** to school.

---

taste Sugar has a sweet **taste.** Lemons have a sour taste.

Baby likes **to taste** any new food before she eats it.
Baby likes **to take a little bite** of any new food before she eats it.

I **tasted** the cake. It tasted good.

---

tea Mother sometimes drinks **tea.** She makes it by putting leaves of a tea plant in hot water. Sometimes she makes it by putting a tea bag in hot water.

teach **Teach** me to read.
Help me **learn** to read.

taught Mother **taught** me to write my name.
She says **teaching** me is fun.

---

teacher My **teacher** at school helps me learn to read. My mother is my teacher in the kitchen. She shows me how to cook.

---

team Charlie Brown and his friends are going to play baseball together. They are a **team.**

A baseball team is made up of nine players.
A football team has eleven players.
A basketball team is made up of five players.

Two horses pulling something **together** are called a **team.**

---

tear Who would want to **tear** Linus's picture?
Who would want to **pull** the picture **apart?**

Someone **tore** the picture because he didn't like it.
Do you suppose the picture was **torn** by Linus himself?

tear

Charlie Brown is crying. His face is wet with **tears.** A **tear** is a **drop of water** that comes out of your eye when you cry.

---

tease We **tease** Sally about the little boy who walks home with her.
We **joke with** Sally about the little boy who walks home with her.

I **tease** my mother to let me go to the circus.
I **ask** my mother **again and again** to let me go to the circus.

Don't tease the kitten. He doesn't like it.

---

teddy bear

Lucy got up to get her **teddy bear.** She likes to take her teddy bear to bed with her. He is soft and pretty. Her teddy bear is her favorite **toy.**

telephone Peppermint Patty is speaking on the **telephone** to someone who is far away. Her voice is carried by a telephone wire to someone who is listening to another telephone at the other end of the wire.

---

television Charlie Brown is watching a show on the **television** set. He sees moving pictures of things happening far away. He hears people talking and singing. Charlie Brown loves to watch **TV.**

tell Do not **tell** where Mother keeps the cookies.
Do not **say** where Mother keeps the cookies.

Violet **told** Lucy a secret.

---

ten There are **ten** cents in a dime.
There are **10** cents in a dime.

Let's count to **ten:**
1 2 3 4 5 6 7 8 9 **10.**

---

tennis **Tennis** is a game played by two or four people. You hit a ball across a net with a special bat called a tennis racket.

---

tent In the summer, the Peanuts bunch goes to camp. They live in the woods in **tents.**

A **tent** looks like a little house made of cloth. A tent is easy to put up anywhere in the summer and can be rolled up and stored in the winter.

Some **tents** are very big. I saw a circus in a big tent.

---

terrible When the two trains hit each other, there was a **terrible** wreck. It **made everyone afraid.**

---

than

Here are three poles. One pole is taller **than** the other two. All three poles are bigger **than** Woodstock.

---

thank When someone does something for you, you say "**Thank** you." When someone gives you something, you say, "Thank you."

We always **thank** people when they do nice things for us.

We write thank you letters for our Christmas gifts.

thankful Linus believes he has many things to thank God for. He is **thankful** to God for making him happy.

---

thanks When we say **"Thanks,"** we mean **"Thank you."** To give thanks means to say "Thank you."

Thanksgiving **Thanksgiving** Day comes in the month of November. Thanksgiving is a **holiday** when we give thanks for many good things.

---

that This is my book, and **that** is your book.
Do you see **that** tree across the street?

Lucy said **that** she wanted to go home.

---

the I don't want just a dog. I want **the** dog we saw in the store. **The** dog we saw was brown with white spots. The other dogs were not as nice as the brown one.

---

theater A **theater** is a building or large room in which we see movies or plays.

their Father and I went to the Joneses' farm.
We went to see **their** horses.
We went to see the horses **that belong to them.**

---

theirs These toys are ours, and the other toys are **theirs.**
These toys are ours, and the other toys **belong to them.**

---

them Your toys are new. Take care of **them.** You will want to play with those toys for a long time.

---

themselves The boys **themselves** said we should not go.
The boys did not need anyone to tell them not to go. They said it on their own.

Sally and Linus were playing by **themselves** away from the others.
Sally and Linus were playing **alone** away from the others.

---

then When Mother calls, **then** I will go home.
When Mother calls, **at that time** I will go home.

First we will go to the movies. **Then** we will have some ice cream.
First we will go to the movies. **Afterward** we will have some ice cream.

there You sit **there** while I go into the store.
You sit **in that place** while I go into the store.

I like to go to the park. Have you ever been **there?**
Have you ever been **to that place?**

There were six candles on my birthday cake.

When I hurt myself, Mother says, **"There, there,** I'll kiss it and make it well."

---

they

Lucy and Linus are at the window. **They** are watching the rain.

The dogs have not eaten today, so **they** are hungry. Schroeder and Roy have been running, so they are very hot.

Mother said, **"They** say we're going to have a hot summer."
Mother said, **"People** say we're going to have a hot summer."

---

thick This wall is **thick.**
This wall is **not thin.**

The grass is tall and **thick** in the meadow.
The grass is tall and **growing close together** in the meadow.

thief A person who steals is a **thief.**

thieves Several **thieves** stole the money, but just one thief was caught.

---

thimble I put a **thimble** over the end of my finger when I sew. I push the needle with that finger. The thimble keeps the needle from sticking my finger. It is made of metal and covers the tip of my finger.

---

thin A piece of paper is **thin.** A wall is thick.

The grass was **thin** on the side of the hill.
The grass was **growing far apart** on the side of the hill.

The dog is **thin.** His bones show under his skin.
The pig is fat. He is round and heavy.

---

thing "What's that **thing** you have there?" asked Charlie Brown. "It's an empty basket," said Snoopy.

What are these **things?**
They are my toys.

Your **things** are all over the floor.
Your clothes and books and toys and papers are all over the floor.

think I **think** with my mind. I must **think** about what to give my mother for Christmas.

I **think** I know where Snoopy is hiding.
I **believe** I know where Snoopy is hiding.

I **thought** of a story that my grandmother used to tell me.

---

third Charlie Brown is **third** in line.
To be third is to be the **number three.**
One of his friends is first in line.
She is number one on the line.
The girl behind her is second.
She is number two in the line.

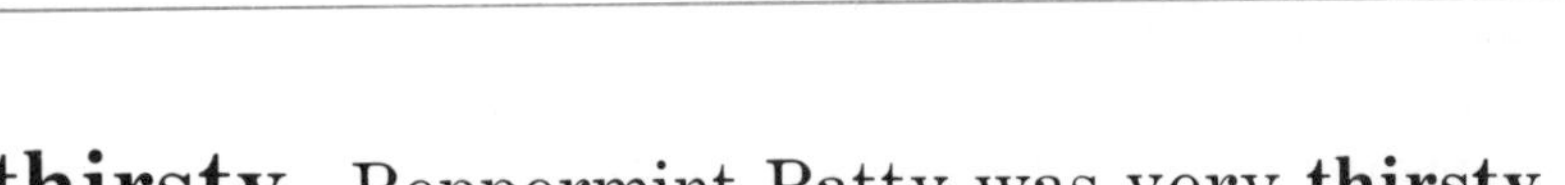

thirsty Peppermint Patty was very **thirsty.**
Her mouth felt dry. When she came upon the water fountain, she drank and drank.

thirty There are **thirty** days in September.
There are **30** days in September.

---

this That apple is yours, but **this** one is mine.
My brother will be six years old **this** week.
This man is my father.

---

those That is his toy, but **those** toys are mine.
Do you see **those** children over there? They are having a party.

---

though My plant will not grow, **though** I water it every day.
My plant will not grow, **even if** I water it every day.

---

thousand Ten times one hundred is one **thousand.**
Ten times 100 is **1,000.**

Fifteen thousand people live in our town.
How many thousand people live in your town?

---

thread Mother sews her dress with **thread.** She uses cotton thread in her needle. Thread is like string, but is very thin.

Can you **thread** the needle?
Can you **put thread through** the needle?

three Charlie Brown, Linus and Thibault are playing hockey.
The **three** of them are playing together.

Three is the number that comes after 2. Let's count to **3:**
1 2 **3.**

---

throat My **throat** is the front of my neck. The inside of my neck is also called my throat. A sore throat is a throat that hurts.

---

through Dad made a hole **through** a penny so that I could put a string in it.
Dad made a hole **from one side to the other side** of a penny so that I could put a string in it.

I read **through** the book.
I read **from beginning to end** of the book.

Frieda is **through** with her work.
Frieda has **finished** with her work.

---

throw

Charlie Brown is ready to **throw** the ball.

He **throws** it to Snoopy.
He **tosses** it straight and high.

He **threw** it too far.
Poor Charlie Brown has not **thrown** the ball right all day.

---

thumb

Charlie Brown hurt his **thumb** opening a can of dog food. The thumb is the thickest finger on each hand. Your fingers bend in two places. Your thumbs bend in only one place.

---

thunder It is going to storm, and I hear a very loud noise from the sky. That is **thunder.** Lightning and thunder often come when we have a rain storm.

Thursday The **fifth day** of the week is **Thursday.**

---

ticket

Charlie Brown and his friends are having a show. To see it, you must buy a **ticket.** You must give this **small card** to someone at the door so you can go into the theater.

You also need a ticket to travel on a train, plane or ship. Your ticket shows that you have paid your fare.

tickle Snoopy likes to have Linus **tickle** his nose. His nose gets a funny feeling when someone scratches it very gently. It makes him want to laugh.

That story **tickles** me.
That story **makes me laugh.**

---

tie

Snoopy is wearing a **tie** around his neck. Daddy wears a tie with his shirt. Their **ties** are made of silk.

The race was a **tie.** The boys came to the end at the same time. Neither won.

When we **tie** a string to a kite, we **connect** the string to the kite. We **make a knot** in the string so that the string and kite will stay joined.

The cowboy **tied** the horse to the fence.
Violet is **tying** a ribbon in her hair.

---

tiger A **tiger** is a large **wild animal.** You may see a tiger in the zoo or at the circus.

tight

Linus's shoes are too **tight.**
They are **too small** for his feet.
They make his feet hurt.

Mother held me **tight** when she kissed me goodbye.
Mother held me **closely** when she kissed me goodbye.

---

till Mother told us we could play outdoors **till** it was dark.
Mother told us we could play outdoors **up to the time** it was dark.

Till means the same as **until.**

---

time Lucy is looking at the clock to see what **time** it is.
It is a minute before four o'clock.

A minute is a short time. A year is a long time.

Eight o'clock is Lucy's bedtime.

I had a good time at the party.

We had to run to be in time for school.
We had to run so that we wouldn't be late.

tin

Snoopy has found an old **tin** can that once held food.
Tin is a **metal** that is often used for food cans.

---

tiny Something **very small** is **tiny.** The bug was so tiny that you could hardly see it.

---

tip The **tip** of a thing is its **very end.** The tip of the arrow is in the tree.

Don't put the glass so near the edge of the table.
It will **tip** over.
It will **fall** over.

---

tiptoe I walked on **tiptoe** down the stairs. I walked **on my toes** so that no one would hear me.

tire Charlie Brown heard the sound of the **tires** on the road and knew the bus was going without him.

Each wheel of a bus is covered by a rubber ring filled with air. This **tire** protects the wheel and makes the bus run smoothly.

Daddy bought four new tires for our car.

---

tired Snoopy is **tired.** He played hard all day and now he needs a rest.

When Daddy is tired, he falls asleep in his chair. When I am tired, I go to bed.

to Go **to** the door and look out.
Go **as far as** the door and look out.

Franklin gave the cookie **to** Schroeder.

I like **to** play outdoors. I do not like **to** stay in the house.

This is the belt **to** my blue coat.
This is the belt **that goes with** my blue coat.

---

toast Charlie Brown and his friends like to **toast** marshmallows.
To **toast** is to **brown with heat.**

They hold the marshmallows near the heat until they are brown.

Linus likes **toast** for breakfast.
Lucy is **toasting** the bread
for him in a toaster.
He likes **toasted** rolls, too.

---

today **Today** is the day that is now. Yesterday is the day before today. Tomorrow is the day after today.

---

toe We have five **toes** on each foot. We can move our toes up and down. We bend our toes when we walk.

The big **toe** is the first toe. It is useful for finding out if the water in the lake is cold.

together Lucy and Charlie Brown are sitting **together** on the bench.
They are sitting **with each other.**

I sewed two pieces of cloth **together.**
I sewed two pieces of cloth **to each other.**

---

tomato A **tomato** is really a **fruit,** but it tastes like a vegetable. Have you ever eaten a ripe, red tomato right out of the garden? That's when **tomatoes** taste best.

---

tomorrow The day after today is **tomorrow.** Today is the day that is now. Yesterday is the day before today.

---

tongue

Linus is sticking out his **tongue.** His tongue should be in his mouth.

We use our **tongues** to speak. Our tongues also help us eat and taste our food.

---

tonight The night of today is **tonight.** Today we do not go to school, and tonight we are going to a movie.

too

Snoopy's collar is **too** big for him.
It is **more than** big **enough** for him.

Woodstock wishes he had a collar **too.**
He wishes he had one **also.**

tool Snoopy came to the **tool** shed to get a tool. A tool is **something that helps us with our work.** There are many kinds of tools. Which tools will Snoopy need to build a new doghouse?

tooth I have a loose **tooth** in my mouth. Soon I will get a new tooth.

teeth When I have all my **teeth,** I will be able to chew my food better.

---

toothbrush Linus brushes his teeth with a **toothbrush** to keep them clean.

---

toothpaste Lucy puts **toothpaste** on her toothbrush when she brushes her teeth. The toothpaste tastes like candy.

---

top Woodstock is sitting on **top** of the tree. He is on the **highest part** of the tree.

Put the **top** on the box. Put the **cover** on the box.

I have a **top** that spins around and around. It's my favorite **toy.**

toss

Why would Snoopy want to **toss** his supper dish away?
Why would he want to **throw** it away?

He is **tossing** his dish because it's empty.
He **tossed** it on the ground.

---

touch "Don't **touch** this paper, Linus," cried Lucy.
"Don't **put a finger** on it!"

Linus **touched** it anyway.

When I walk on tiptoe, my heels don't touch the floor.
When heat touches snow, the snow melts.

---

toward I am going **toward** the park. If I keep on going the way I am, I will get to the park.

---

towards **Towards** means **toward.**

---

towel When Charlie Brown takes a bath, he dries his body with a bath **towel.** I dry my hands on a hand towel. Mother dries the dishes with a dish towel. A towel is a piece of cloth used to dry something.

tower The tall, narrow part of a building is a **tower.** Have you ever seen a church tower?

---

town A **town** is a **small city.** We do not live in a town. We live in the country.

---

toy

Linus has a **toy** truck. It is not a real truck. It is a thing that he plays with.

Linus and Lucy have many **toys.** They play with their toys in their bedroom.

---

track A railroad **track** is the road the trains run on. It is made of iron rails.

When an animal walks in the snow or mud, he leaves the marks of his feet. I saw rabbit **tracks** in the snow.

The Indians know how **to track** animals.
The Indians know how **to follow** the tracks of animals.

tractor A **tractor** is a big machine that can pull heavy things. The farmer uses his tractor to pull his plow and do other work on the farm.

---

trade I will **trade** books with you. I will give you my book if you will give me your book.

We **trade** with Mr. Jones.
We **buy from** Mr. Jones.

---

trailer I saw a car with a **trailer** on it. The trailer was like a room on wheels. People could sleep in it at night.

Some **trailers** are used to carry loads.

---

train A **train** is a row of railroad cars pulled by an engine.

---

trap A **trap** is used to catch animals. We caught a mouse in a mousetrap.

He **trapped** me into telling my secret.
He **tricked** me into telling my secret.

---

travel I like to **travel.**
I like to **go from one place to another.** I like to travel by airplane.

treat Mother took us to the circus for a **treat.** Another treat was the lemonade and peanuts we had to eat. A treat is **something pleasant.**

I'll **treat** you to a dish of ice cream.
I'll **buy** you a dish of ice cream **for a present.**

You must always **treat** your pets well.
You must always **act** well **toward** your pets.

My aunt **treated** me like a big boy when she came to see us.

---

tree "Look, Linus," said Charlie Brown. "The **trees** are beginning to bloom."

A **tree** is a **very big plant.** The tree trunk is wood. A tree has branches and leaves. There are many kinds of trees. Some are green only in summer. Some are green all the year round.

---

trick Lucy played a **trick** on Charlie Brown.

It wasn't nice of Lucy **to trick** him.
It wasn't nice of Lucy **to fool** Charlie Brown.

My dog can do a trick.
My dog can walk on his hind legs.

---

trim We will **trim** the Christmas tree. We will make it look pretty with lights and shiny balls and strips of silver paper.

Father can **trim** the dog's hair.
Father can **cut a little bit off** the dog's hair.

Uncle John has his hair **trimmed** every two weeks.

Mother is **trimming** my dress with white lace.
Trimming is something put on a dress to make it look prettier.

trip

Snoopy is going on a **trip.**
He is **going** someplace **away** from home.

Watch where you're going, or you will **trip.**
You'll catch your foot on something and **start to fall.**

I almost **tripped** over your suitcase.

---

trouble Kitty causes **trouble** when she pushes the sewing basket over.
Kitty causes **bother** for all of us when she pushes the sewing basket over.

If you are naughty, you may get into trouble.
Something that is not pleasant may happen to you.

trousers He has his first pair of long **trousers.**
He has his first pair of long **pants.**

---

truck Linus has a toy **truck.** It is carrying a load of sand. Real trucks are larger than automobiles and are made to carry heavy loads.

---

true It is **true** that two and two are four. It is true that the world is round. It is true that the sun rises in the east. Anything that is true is **not a lie.**

---

trunk Snoopy has just arrived at camp with his **trunk.** All his things are packed in the trunk. A trunk is larger than a suitcase.

The lower part of a tree is called a **trunk.** A tree trunk is wood.

An elephant's long nose is called a **trunk.**

trust I **trust** you. I believe that you are honest. I believe that you will do as you say.

---

truth Always tell the **truth.**
Always tell **things that are true.**

---

try I **try** to be a good child. I will try to remember everything in my lesson. I do all I can to remember.

Why don't you try the book and see if you like it?

I **tried** to ride my bicycle down the hill, but it was too steep.
Charlie Brown is **trying** to get his work done early so that he can go to the movies.

---

tub We bathe in a **bathtub.** We wash our clothes in a wash tub. The farmer sold us a tub of butter. **An open container** is a **tub.**

Tuesday **Tuesday** is the **third day** of the week.

---

tulip A **tulip** is a **flower.** It blooms in the spring.

---

tumble Baby's **tumble** off the chair made him cry.
Baby's **fall** off the chair made him cry.

When we're playing at the farm, we **tumble** in the hay.
When we're playing at the farm, we **bounce around** in the hay.

Tumbling is fun.
I **tumbled** into bed at the end of the day.

---

tunnel A **tunnel** is a long hole under the ground or snow. We made a tunnel in the deep snow. Then we crawled into one end of it and came out the other end.

A railroad train often goes through a tunnel.

---

turkey A **turkey** is a **large bird.** We like to eat turkey when Mother roasts it. We have turkey for Thanksgiving dinner.

---

turn

Watch out, Charlie Brown! Snoopy is going to **turn.**

He is **turning** around and going back where he started.

Snoopy has had his **turn** on the skate board. Now it is Charlie Brown's chance.

It is supposed to **turn** cold tonight.
It is supposed to **become** cold.

I **turned** off the lights when I went to bed.

---

turnip A **turnip** is a **vegetable** that grows in the garden. The part of the turnip that we eat is the root.

turtle We saw a **turtle** walking by the side of the road. We saw another turtle turned on his back. A turtle has a hard shell on his back. **Turtles** are **animals** that move slowly.

---

twelve **Twelve** is a number that looks like this: **12.** There are twelve inches in a foot. Let's count to **12:**
1 2 3 4 5 6 7 8 9 10 11 **12.**

---

twenty **Twenty** is a number that looks like this: **20.** If you count all your fingers and your toes, you will have **20** altogether.

---

twenty-five **Twenty-five** is a number that looks like this: **25.** There are **25** cents in a quarter.

---

twice I am **twice** as old as he is.
I am **two times** as old as he is. I am eight years old. He is four years old.

---

twin Two children who have the same mother and were born at the same time are **twins.** Twins often look alike.

twinkle The stars **twinkle** at night.
The stars **seem to give off flashes of light** at night.

---

two **Two** is the number that follows one.

Charlie Brown has opened two cans of dog food.
First he opened one. Then he opened another one.
1 + 1 make 2.

U u

ugly

Charlie Brown tried to scare Frieda by making an **ugly** face at her. He made a face that was **not pleasant to look at.**

The bad man in the movie sounded **ugly.** He sounded **mean and angry.**

umbrella When Peppermint Patty walks in the rain, she holds an **umbrella** over her head. The rain falls on the umbrella and she stays dry underneath it.

uncle Your father's brother is your **uncle.** Your mother's brother is your uncle. Your aunt's husband is your uncle.

under Linus puts his book **under** his pillow. He puts it **beneath** his pillow. The pillow is on top of the book.

understand

Snoopy does not **understand** why he's in the doctor's office. He does not **know why** he is there.

Charlie Brown said, "Let's go." That Snoopy **understood.**

---

undress Charlie Brown must **undress** to take a bath.
He must **take his clothes off.**

He **undressed** in a hurry.

---

unhappy

Sally Brown is **unhappy** because she doesn't want to go to school.
She is **sad** because she doesn't want to go to school.

---

uniform Snoopy is wearing a soldier's **uniform.**
He is wearing a **special kind of suit** and hat that only soldiers wear.

Policemen wear uniforms too.

United Nations The **United Nations** is a group of many countries. It is working to stop wars and make people safe all over the world.

United States of America The **United States of America** is a big country. There are fifty states in the United States of America. The flag of the **U.S.A.** is red, white and blue.

unless I will come to your house **unless** my mother says no.
I will come to your house **if** my mother does **not** say no.

---

untie When I put my shoes on, I tie the laces of my shoes.
When I take my shoes off, I **untie** my shoelaces.
I open the knots in my laces.

---

until I will stay here **until** Mother calls me.
I will stay here **up to the time** Mother calls me.

---

up

Sally and Linus are looking **up** at an airplane. It is high above them.

We walked **up** the hill.
We walked **to a higher part** of the hill.

---

upon Snoopy is **upon** the roof.
He is sitting **on** the roof.

---

upside down

Look at Woodstock.
His head is down and his feet are up. He is **upside down.**

---

upstairs My bedroom is **upstairs.**
My bedroom is **on a higher floor.**

Charlie Brown chased Snoopy **upstairs.**
Charlie Brown chased Snoopy **up the stairs.**

us

"Oh boy," thought Snoopy. The three of **us** are going to have supper together."
Snoopy means that Charlie Brown, Linus and he are going to have supper together.

Us always means **myself** and **somebody else.**

---

use "I can't write this story," says Charlie Brown. "There's no **use** in trying. It would not be time spent well."

Use your head, Charlie Brown. **Put** your mind **to work.**

I **use** my feet for walking. I **use** my eyes for seeing.
I **used** my shovel to dig in the sand.

I **used** to live in the country. **Before now** I lived in the country.

I am **used** to getting up early. I do it all the time.

The paint is all **used** up. There is no more left.

---

useful This book is **useful.** I learn many things from it. My pen and pencil are useful. I write with them. My rubbers are useful. They keep my feet dry in wet weather. All these things help me.

V v

vacation A child's **vacation** is the time he does not go to school. We will visit Grandmother during Christmas vacation.

A grownup's vacation is the time he does not go to work. Our whole family will go on a trip during my dad's vacation.

valentine

Here is a **valentine** from Charlie Brown. We send letters and cards to our friends on Valentine's Day to remind them that we love them.

valley The **valley** is the land between the hills.

vegetable A **vegetable** is a **plant that is used for food.** A potato is a vegetable. Other vegetables are corn, cabbage, beans, carrots and beets.

very Woodstock is **very** tired. He is so tired that he can't do anything but sleep. He is so very tired that Snoopy cannot wake him up. He'll wake up after a long nap.

village A **village** is a small town. There are only a few houses and a few stores in the village where we live.

vine A plant that grows along the ground is a **vine.** A plant that climbs up a wall or a tree is a vine. A pumpkin vine grows on the ground. Some vines grow on walls.

violet A **violet** is a **flower.** It grows in the shade.

Violet is a **color** like purple. Violet is a pretty name for a girl.

violin A **violin** is a **musical instrument.** A violin has strings that make music when you touch them.

visit Charlie Brown has come to **visit** Schroeder. He has come to see Schroeder and stay to talk to him for a while.

They had a nice visit.
Then Charlie Brown went home.

visitor When you visit someone, you are a **visitor.** We had a visitor at our house today. My mother and I were visitors at my aunt's house last week.

voice **The sound I make with my mouth** is my **voice.** I talk with my voice. I sing with my voice. I yell with my voice.

wade I can **wade** up to my knees.
I can **walk in the water** up to my knees.

wag If Snoopy is happy, he will **wag** his tail.
He will **wave** his tail **from side to side.**

wagon

Linus has a little **wagon.**
His wagon has four wheels and a handle to pull it by.
Sometimes he gives Snoopy a ride in his wagon.

waist The part of your body that you put your belt around is your **waist.**

wait "**Wait** a minute," said Sally. "Stay where you are. A car is coming."
Charlie Brown and Sally **waited** until the car went by.
Many people were **waiting** for the bus.

A nice lady **waited** on us in the restaurant. She brought us our lunch.

wake **Wake** up, Snoopy. **Stop sleeping.** Linus and Charlie Brown have come to play.

woke Snoopy **woke** up slowly. It took a few minutes before he became awake.

---

walk

Linus is taking a **walk** to Charlie Brown's house. He must **walk** because he could not get a ride. He has to **go along on his own two feet.**

Linus doesn't really mind **walking.**
He **walked** downtown and back yesterday.

---

wall Charlie Brown is thinking he may climb a **wall.** This wall is made of bricks and it is very thick and strong. It goes around the yard like a fence.

The outside **walls** of our house are made of stone.
There is wallpaper on the walls of my room.

want

"Hey, Charlie Brown do you **want** a bite of my ice cream cone?"
Charlie Brown would **like to have** some ice cream, but he **wants** some of his own.

He **wanted** to buy some, but he didn't have any money.

He was **in want** of money.
He **needed** some money.

---

war A **war** is a fight between countries. The army fights in a war on land. The navy fights in a war on the sea.

---

warm When I stand near the fire, I am **warm.** When I stand too near the fire, I am **hot.**

It is **warm** in the sunshine. It is cool in the shade of a tree.

I wear **warm** mittens in the winter.
I wear mittens **that keep me warm** in the winter.

wash It's Snoopy's job to **wash** the dishes.
He must **clean** each dish **with soap and water.**

Snoopy does not like **washing** dishes.

I **washed** my hands and face before dinner.

We do our **wash** on Monday.
We wash our clothes on Monday.

waste We must never **waste** food.
We must never use food so that a part of it will have to be thrown away.

We must never waste money.
We must never spend money so that we get nothing good for it.

---

watch Linus is wearing a **watch** on his wrist. His watch tells him what time it is.

Watch me jump over the chair.
Look at me jump over the chair.

We'll **watch for** Daddy's car to come down the street.
We'll **look for** Daddy's car to come down the street.

Watch out that you don't fall down.
Be careful that you don't fall down.

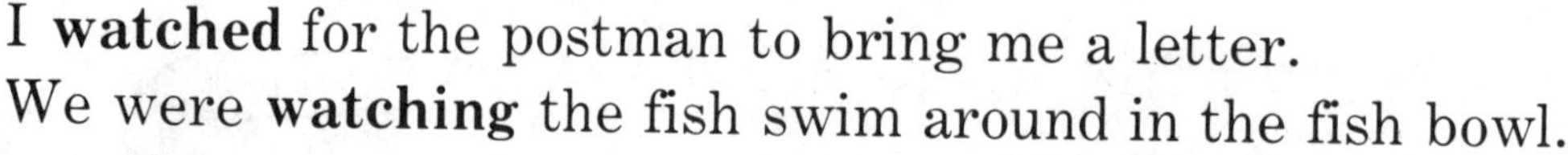

I **watched** for the postman to bring me a letter.
We were **watching** the fish swim around in the fish bowl.

---

water We drink **water.** We wash in water. The rivers and lakes and oceans are filled with water. Water is a liquid.

Mother is going **to water** her plants.
Mother is going **to put water** on her plants.

---

watermelon A **watermelon** is a very large **fruit.** Watermelons are full of sweet juice. They have many seeds. They grow in the fields on vines.

wave A big ocean **wave** is carrying Snoopy to shore. Snoopy loves to play in the waves.

I always **wave** goodbye to Daddy when he leaves the house.

The flag is **waving** in the wind.
The policeman **waved** his hand to tell the cars to move on.

---

wax Candles are made of **wax.** The wax melts as the candles burn.

Mother puts **wax** on the floor. Then she rubs it to make the floor shine.

---

way

Charlie Brown kicked a can that was in his **way.**
The can was in his **path.**

My house is a long **way** from school.
My house is **very far** from school.

This is the **way** I brush my hair.
This is **how** I brush my hair.

Which **way** is the grocery store?
How do I **get to** the grocery store?

---

we When I talk about myself and some others, I use the word **we.** When Lucy and Linus and I left home, it was raining. We had umbrellas, so we didn't get wet.

weak When I was sick, I was **weak** and had to stay in bed.
When I was sick, I was **not strong** and had to stay in bed.

Daddy doesn't like weak tea.

---

wear The children **wear** funny clothes for Halloween.
They **are dressed** in sheets.

Snoopy is not **wearing** a costume.

He **wore** his pilot's hat last Halloween, but he has not **worn** it since.

---

weather The **weather** is wet. It's raining hard. Yesterday the weather was good. The sun was shining and the sky was clear.

In the summer, the **weather** is warm.
In the summer, the **air outdoors** is warm.

Wednesday The **fourth day** of the week is **Wednesday.**

---

week A **week** is made up of **seven days.** The days of the week are Sunday, Monday, Tuesday, Wednesday, Thursday, Friday and Saturday. There are four weeks in a month.
There are fifty-two weeks in a year.

weigh To **weigh** is to measure how heavy a thing is.
I weigh fifty pounds.

---

weight How heavy are you? What is your **weight?** Your weight is measured in pounds. Charlie Brown's weight is fifty-three pounds.

---

welcome "**Welcome** to my house," said Linus.
"I'm glad to have you here."

"Thank you," said Lucy.
"You're **welcome,**" said Linus.

---

well Are you **well** today?
Are you **in good health** today?

Schroeder plays the piano **well.** He is **good at** playing the piano.

At the farm we get water from a **well.**
At the farm we get water from a **deep hole in the ground.**

---

we'll **We'll** means **we will.** I hope we'll see you again soon.

---

west If you look at the sun as it goes down in the evening, you will be looking **west.** West is to your left on a map when you read it.

wet Charlie Brown is all **wet**.
The fountain sprayed water all over him.

---

what **What** are you doing? Tell me the thing you are doing.
What kind of animal is that? Tell me about that animal.
What shall we have for dinner? Tell me about dinner.

---

what's **What's** means **what is.** What's the matter?

---

wheat You can see **wheat** growing in the field. The grains of wheat are ground into flour, and the flour is made into bread.

---

wheel

A **wheel** is round, and is usually made of wood or metal. A wheel makes things move. Linus's skate board has wheels. As the wheels turn round and round, the skate board moves along the ground.

---

when Do you know **when** Mother will be home?
Do you know **at what time** Mother will be home?

---

whenever I will meet you **whenever** you tell me to.
I will meet you **at any time** you tell me to.

where **Where** do you live?
In what place do you live?

---

whether I don't know **whether** to put a red dress or a blue dress on my doll. I don't know **if** I should use the red dress or the blue dress.
I don't know which of the two dresses to choose.

I must go to school whether it rains or not.

---

which That is the story **which** our teacher reads to us.

Which one of the hats is yours?

If you could travel by train or airplane, **which** one would you choose? **Which** way would you rather go?

---

while I will work **while** you play.
I will work **at the same time** that you play.

He waited **a while** for his father to come.
He waited **a time** for his father to come.

---

whisper Sally has a secret to tell Charlie Brown. She speaks in a **whisper,** because she doesn't want anyone else to hear. She speaks in a **very soft voice.**

We whisper when we want to speak very quietly.

The teacher said, "No **whispering** while you are in the classroom."
No one **whispered** after that.

whistle

I can **whistle.**
I can make a sound when I blow air through my lips.

Snoopy has a **whistle.** When he blows into it, it makes a loud, high noise.

---

white **White** is the **color** of snow. Ducks have white feathers. The sheets on my bed are white. Marshmallows are white.

---

who **Who** is this boy beside us? **Who** are those children over there? This is the friend **who** went with me. And these are the others **who** stayed home.

---

whole The **whole** of anything is **all of** it. Charlie Brown ate the whole cake. He didn't leave even one piece of it.

---

whom The girl to **whom** I waved is my best friend.

whose **Whose** dog is this? To whom does it belong?

---

why Do you know **why** it is so cold today?
Do you know **the reason** that it is so cold today?

---

wide Lucy's mouth is **wide** open. It is open all the way.

The road was **wide.** It was **not narrow.**

I measured our door. It is two feet **wide.**

---

wife A married woman is a **wife.** A married man is a husband.
My mother is my father's wife.

wild The **wild** animals live in the fields and woods. They run away and hide when you go near them. A cat is a tame animal that lives in the house. A bear is a wild animal.

Mother says, "Sometimes the children are too wild. They run and shout too much."

The wind tonight is wild. It is as strong and fierce as a tiger.

---

will I **will** come to see you tomorrow. My aunt will visit us for a week. Mother will take Baby for a walk after his nap.

would Violet **would** like to go to the movies. Would you go with her?

I would help you if I could.

won't **Won't** means **will not.** I won't go with you.

wouldn't **Wouldn't** means **would not.** I wouldn't do that if I were you.

---

willow A **willow** tree grows near our house.

---

win To **win** you must do better than anyone else who is trying to do the same thing. I hope I will win the race.

won I **won** the race.

---

wind Can you **wind** the string into a ball?
Can you **turn** the string **around into a ball?**

wind

The **wind** blew so hard it took Linus's blanket away. The wind is moving air. We call a soft wind a breeze. We call a strong wind a windstorm.

---

windy

It is a very **windy** day. The wind is blowing hard. It blows Linus's hair back. It blows at his blanket. It blows the leaves off the trees.

---

window Lucy is looking out of the **window.** Even though the window is closed, she can see through the glass. We open the window to let fresh air in. We close the window to keep cold air out.

---

wing A bird's **wing** is covered with feathers. A bird moves his two wings when he flies through the air. The wings are to fly with.

The **wings** of an airplane hold it up in the air.

---

winter **Winter** is one of the four **seasons** of the year. Autumn, spring and summer are the other seasons. In some parts of the United States of America there is snow in the winter.

wipe When I wash my face, I **wipe** it with a towel.
When I wash my face, I **rub** it dry with a towel.

I wipe my muddy shoes before I come into the house.
I wipe the dishes for Mother.

---

wire

The fence behind Peppermint Patty and Charlie Brown is made of one kind of **wire.** Wire looks like rope or string made of metal that you can bend.

Another kind of wire is a telephone wire that carries our voices from one place to another. Electric wires bring electricity into our house.

---

wish Lucy must stay in the house. "I **wish** I could go out," she says.
"I want to go out."

When you blow out your birthday candles, you make a **wish.**
You **wish** for something nice to happen.
You **hope** something nice will happen.

I am **wishing** for a new doll.
I **wished** it would stop raining. The good fairy said, "You may have three **wishes.**"

witch

Lucy is dressed up like a **witch.** A witch is supposed to ride on a broomstick and do magic things. We read about witches in stories, but witches are just make-believe. A witch is not a real person.

---

with I am going **with** my daddy to the farm. We are going together. I like my new dress **with** the lace trimming.

We eat **with** a knife and fork. We **use** them.

My teacher is pleased **with** my good work.

---

within I will be there **within** a half hour.
I will be there **in not more than** a half hour.

---

without Daddy ran out **without** a hat.
Daddy ran out **with no** hat.

---

wolf A **wolf** is a **wild animal.** It looks like a big dog.

wolves There are still some **wolves** in the west part of the United States of America and in Canada.

woman My mother is a **woman.** My daddy is a man. A girl grows up to be a woman.

women There were several **women** at the party.

---

wonder I **wonder** what is wrong with my toy train. I **ask myself** what is wrong with my toy train. It will not run.

I wonder if I can fix my toy train by myself. Maybe Father will help me fix it. I wonder if we can make it run again.

No wonder Baby can't talk. She's too young. **It is not a surprise** that Baby can't talk. She's too young.

---

wonderful It was **wonderful** to see the country from an airplane. It was so beautiful, I will never forget it.

---

wood

Charlie Brown's baseball bats are made of **wood.** The bench is made of wood. So is the fence. We cut down trees to get wood. Then we make it into many useful things. Even houses are often made of wood.

---

wooden **Wooden** means **made of wood.** In some countries, people wear wooden shoes.

woodpecker A **woodpecker** is a **bird** with a long sharp bill. He pecks holes in trees to get bugs to eat.

---

woods We went for a walk in the **woods.**
We walked to a place where there were many trees growing close together.

The woods are cool and shady. Squirrels and rabbits and other animals live in the woods.

---

wool **Wool** is the fur that grows on sheep. The sheep's wool is cut off and made into wool cloth. The wool cloth is then made into clothes, blankets and other things. When I go out to play in the winter, I wear a wool coat and wool mittens.

---

woolen **Woolen** means made of wool.

---

word Each **word** in this book is explained. We use words to talk with. We use words when we write. When we read, we know what the words mean.

---

work My **work** is to help Mother clean the house.
I like to work. When I do not work, I play or rest.

I **worked** all morning cutting the grass.
My father is not **working** today. It is Sunday.
My brother **works** after school delivering newspapers.

world The whole earth and the sky is the **world.** Linus is looking at a special round map of the world called a globe. The world is round.

---

worm A **worm** is a creature that moves by crawling on the ground. Worms live in holes in the ground. Birds dig for worms to eat.

---

worry Something is making Charlie Brown **worry.**

He is **troubled in his mind.**

He is **worrying** because he didn't do his school work.
He is **worried** about what his teacher will say when she finds out.

---

worse My dog has been sick. He is **worse** today.
My dog has been sick. He is **more sick** today.

My kitty was bad, but yours acted **worse.**
My kitty was bad, but yours acted even **more badly.**

---

worth Mother bought a dollar's **worth** of meat. The meat **cost** a dollar.

That book is not **worth** reading.
That book is not **good enough** for reading.

This toy is worth one dollar. It cost one dollar.

---

wrap

Linus is trying to **wrap** a package. He covers the box with paper, then ties a ribbon around it.

Now the package is **wrapped.**
Linus likes **wrapping** packages.

wreck I saw an automobile **wreck.** The automobile was **all broken.**

Don't **wreck** my house of blocks.
Don't **break up** my house of blocks.

wren A little **wren** sat on a branch outside my window. It was a little **bird** singing a loud, sweet song.

wrist My **wrist** is between my hand and my arm. I can turn my hand on my wrist. Mother wears a watch around her wrist.

write Charlie Brown is helping Linus to **write** a letter.
He is helping him **put words and letters on paper.**

Linus is **writing** with a pencil.
Most letters are **written** with a pen and ink.
When Linus finished his letter, he **wrote** his name on the bottom.

wrong I put my gloves on the **wrong** hands. They are **not** on **right.**

It is **wrong** to lie. It is right to tell the truth.

X x

xylophone A **xylophone** is a **musical instrument.** It has rows of bars of different sizes. The bars are struck with wooden hammers and each bar makes a different sound.

Y y

yard Charlie Brown is playing in his **yard.** He is playing on the **ground around his house.**

I have a **yard** of ribbon.
I have a **piece** of ribbon **three feet long.**

yarn Wool is sometimes made into **yarn.**
Wool is sometimes made into **long threads.** Cotton and silk are also made into yarn.

Mother is making a sweater with wool yarn.

year There are twelve months in a **year.** They are January, February, March, April, May, June, July, August, September, October, November and December.

I am five **years** old. My brother is seven years old.

yell No one can **yell** like Lucy.
No one can **shout** louder than Lucy.

When she lets out a **yell,** Linus's hair stands up because he is afraid.

"Stop **yelling,** Lucy," he says.
"I hate being **yelled** at."

---

yellow Yellow is a light, bright **color.** Butter is yellow. A dandelion is yellow. A lemon is a yellow fruit.

---

yes Daddy asked if I wanted to go to town. I said, **"Yes,** I do."

To say **"yes"** is to agree. "Yes, Snoopy, I will play with you."

---

yesterday The day before today was **yesterday.** Today is the day that is now. Tomorrow is the day after today.

---

yet I haven't combed my hair **yet.**
I haven't combed my hair **up till now.**

Don't take off your coat **yet.**
Don't take off your coat **this soon.**

That dog is barking **yet.**
That dog is barking **still.**

I ran as fast as I could, **yet** I could not catch him.
I ran as fast as I could, **but** I could not catch him

---

you **You** can mean one person or more than one person. The teacher said to the children, "Are you all here?" Then Schroeder came into the room. She said, "Oh, there you are, Schroeder."

you'll **You'll** means **you will.** I think you'll like my new coat.

---

young

Linus is a **young** boy. He is only seven years old. He is still a child. He is not old like Grandfather. Grandfather is seventy-five.

---

your This is **your** toothbrush and **your** toothpaste, Charlie Brown. They **belong to you.**

---

you're **You are** and **you're** mean the same thing. I think you're very smart.

---

yours That hat is **yours.**
That hat **belongs to you.**

---

yourself If I leave you, you will be by **yourself.**
If I leave you, you will be **alone.**

Did you stick **yourself** with the needle?

You **yourself** should keep your room neat.

Z z

zebra A **zebra** is an **animal** with dark and white stripes on its body. The zebra is about as big as a small horse.

zero **Zero** means **none** or **nothing.** This is called a zero: **0.**

When people say, "It's almost zero today," they mean that it is very cold outdoors.

zoo I like to go to the **zoo** and see the animals. The animals that live in the zoo come from all parts of the world. Some wild animals are brought to the zoo. They are kept in cages so they can't hurt anybody.